HARDPRESS.NET
HOME OF HARD-TO-FIND BOOKS

Sporting Scenes and Sundry Sketches
by J. Cypress

Address:
HardPress
8345 NW 66TH ST #2561
MIAMI FL 33166-2626
USA
Email: info@hardpress.net

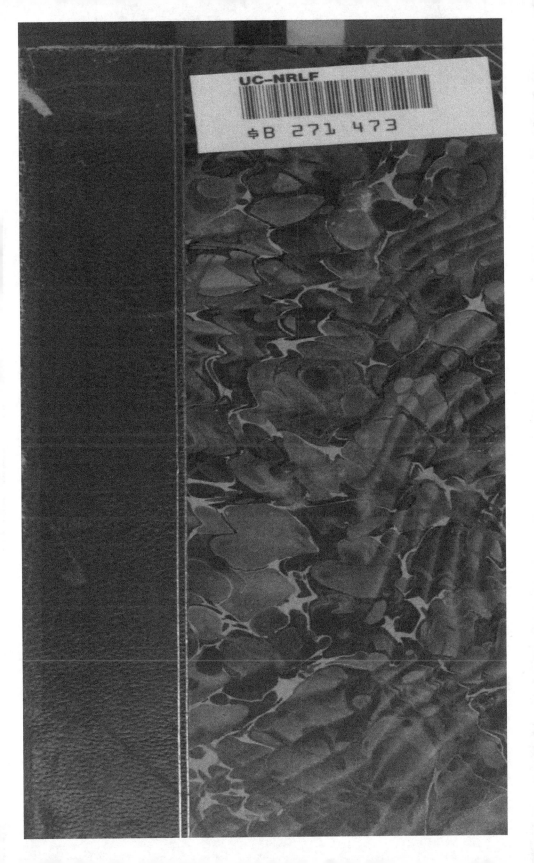

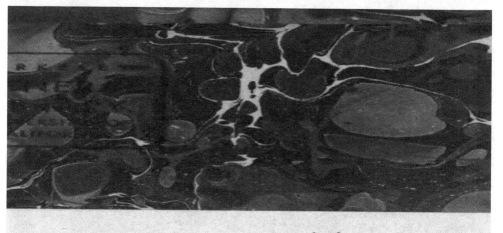

LUX ET

VERITAS

EX-LIBRIS

ARTHUR
FAIRFIELD
GRAY

SPORTING SCENES

AND

SUNDRY SKETCHES.

SPORTING SCENES

AND

SUNDRY SKETCHES.

SPORTING SCENES

AND

SUNDRY SKETCHES;

BEING THE

MISCELLANEOUS WRITINGS

OF

J. CYPRESS, JR.

Wm. P. Hawes

EDITED BY
FRANK FORESTER.

IN TWO VOLUMES.
VOL. II.

NEW YORK:
PUBLISHED BY GOULD, BANKS & Co.
NO. 144 NASSAU STREET.

1842.

ALEXANDER S. GOULD, PRINTER,
No. 144 Nassau Street, New York.

CONTENTS

OF VOLUME II.

CLASSIC RHAPSODIES.

CLASSIC RHAPSODIES.

NO. I.

THE RAPTURE OF PROSERPINE.

A RHAPSODY, FROM OVID.

THE INFLICTION.

THE thunderbolts of Jove had triumphed, and impious Typhæus stretched his prostrate length along the groaning earth. Glad Sicily was laid upon the conquered monster, to keep him down ; for Jupiter knew well enough there 'd be another bloody fight, if ever he got up. Upon his hundred heads rested alarmed old Ætna, covering all save a few long straggling locks. The imposition of such heavy weight, of stone, and wood, and water, bore not the vanquished foe, with dutiful submission ; bore not the inhumation, and thanked the hand that buried him ; but up against the blackened sky, ingrate, from his rebellious bowels, belched such showers of ashes, and clouds of smoke, mixed up with lava and lumps of coke, that Ocean roared with fear, and Ætna's peaceful seats reeled, and rolled, to and fro, with terror and dismay.

The God of Tartarus upstarted at the din, heard in his house profound, all trembling, lest his roof should suddenly be cracked, and daylight enter, and the ghosts get out, and he be overwhelmed with suits for the escape. Up ! up ! thou wary jailor ! He harnessed his black steeds, into his chariot sprang, shook the loose reins, cracked his long lash,—of cast off secondary lightning, twisted, his brother Jove's last new-year's present,——and drove, impetuous, up to earth, to see what in the d——l's name could be to pay.

Up to the regions of sunshine and day his coursers soon galloped, running, with reckless leaps, their rude, rough way. And now they stamp Trinacrian ground, and climb old Ætna's dizzy steep, and snuff the tainted air, and paw the yet warm sulphur, wandering at will ; while Pluto, far aloft, from peak to peak springs anxious, thoughtful, surveying cracks, chasms, and craters.

Within a bower, on Ida's side, the Cytherean goddess slept ——her cherished trysting place of old, when good Anchises was a juvenal. The dusky form of Pluto, leaping over the hills, threw its long shadow on the peaceful grove. The shadow, and the form, dismal, and cold, and grim, awoke the jealous queen, awoke to call her archer boy, with summons quick and shrill. "Eros! my son! Cupid! fly quick! Hither! come hither!"

Cupid was frolicking, down in a vale, busy, as usual, sticking a pin in the breast of a captive beetle. He ran to his mother, and buried his head in her bosom.

"If ever thou did'st love me, boy ; if in thy gentle mother's breast thou hast delight, and dreamy joy, pillowed, in deep and balmy rest ; be now my grateful Eros, my darling avenger ; our long insulted shrines are thirsting for vengeance on Pluto's chill philosophy,——his haughty heart,——his stubborn knee, that bends not—owns not woman, nor me ;——thine is the grace, to bring yon reprobate to know, redeemed, a Benedict's condition ; to bid him at my footstool kneel, the pangs of torturing love to feel, fearing, hoping, wishing. But now, he treads the withering earth, secure in pride of regal birth, and spurns the joys of woman's arms, rejects her love, derides her charms; the murky craven! By Styx! the old cold-hearted rip deserts for whiskey, rum, and flip, the eye, the brow, the cheek, the lip, replete with happy heaven! And shall we then confess, conquered, despised, our power is less than haughty Pluto's? What! has high heaven confessed a rape, and shall low Erebus escape, and we excuse the duty which the brute owes! No! bring your bow and arrows!

It was a goodly sight to see the queen of beauty, with flushed and anxious face, hurry and help the god of love. It was a goodly sound to hear, with voice subdued, but accents clear, queen Venus cheer her son. "Shoot! till he feels the glowing flame; shoot! for your mother's glorious fame; shoot! for the honor of your name, love, and love's archery."

"Your word is law, good mother," said fun-loving Cupid, unbuckling his quiver. "Your breath upon this arrow. I'll do the business for the old bachelor in a twinkling. Speak softly, on this barb, her name whom he shall love."

The goddess kissed its point—the pain-and-pleasure-bearing weapon—and smoothed its plume upon her billowy bosom. The dart was keen, and strait, and truly balanced, and Paphia approved it, and whispered, on its edge, the name of "*Proserpine*," and laid it in the rest.

There was a fixing, a bending, a tension, a pulling of a bowstring, a twang, a slip, and a whiz through the air, and it straight was all over with Pluto.

"Ha! ha! look! look! mamma, ha! ha!" Cupid laughed heartily, seeing the arrow quivering in Pluto's heart, and hearing him swear, "By Orcus! what a sudden stitch I've got in my left side!" "The gentleman from Styx is stuck," pursued my lord of love, merry as a cricket; "the judge of

1*

Tartarus has caught a 'Tartar.   Charon's old master has a new care on his royal hands to manage."

"Stop your nonsense, you monkey!" said Venus, hitting the boy with her fan, "and bend your saucy knees, in love-suits ever suppliant and successful, and wrestle with Olympus, and move all gods to send the daughter of the wheat-and-indian lady before his lovesick eyes? for if she be not seen, our vengeance half is lost, and your great-uncle, there, will soon go down to Erebus, not knowing whence or what the pains that rack his frame.

"This cursed climate," Pluto cried, deep sighing, to himself, "delights not our condition; so rough, so raw, so cold, and soon, again, so hot.   I must be off, and seek in regions more congenial, a steadier sky and heat more equable.   This long old giant here lies quietly enough, and I hope he'll not raise such a rumpus again.—Alas! my side! my side!"

With such soliloquy, he nourished his deep wound, nor knew the secret cause of his distress; knew not the subtle venom that swelled his starting veins; knew not the glorious agony from ordinary pains.   His coursers feel the lash, burning their trembling flanks.   Now, onward, and away!—they spring, they rear, they rush, bearing their sorrowful master.

And soon, before his wonder-smitten eyes, deep, dimpling, pure, and cool, old Pergus lies, and lifts, upon his silver, crystal wave, the songs of snowy swans, that wanton, lave their spotless plumes, and swim, and swimming, sing, arch the the proud neck, and curve the sounding wing.   A grove, impervious, crowns the lake, hanging above the cherished water, and, sacred, guards with veil opaque the virgin revelry of Ceres' daughter.   There is she now, with her maidens, adjusting her long hair, gazing into the mirror of that lake, and humming to herself a sweet low tune.   Her maidens, all around, are gathering fragrant flowers ; and flowers, and girls, and buds, and blossoms, are mingled all together, in a confused perplexing mass of beauty.

But O !the m istress of that troupe, how beautiful was she ! And that strange gazer on the group, how suddenly crazed was he ! Young Proserpine was flattered by Pluto's wild confusion, and moved with more coquettish grace, and from her eyes shot rays more brilliant, when, with half averted head, she saw the royal stranger, bewildered by swans' songs, and maidens' voices, rein up his coursers with a sudden jerk, that brought them on their haunches. The dallying breeze blew back the light transparent folds of her thin stola, and played with her brown ringlets, and lifted up her neckerchief from off her full deep bosom ; up and down, up and down, how heaved that beautiful bosom !

The kingly lover gazed, and drank the subtle poison ; drank and gazed, gazed and drank, and gazed and drank on still. His parched tongue and lips refuse their usual function ; staring he sat, and dumb. So, bloodless, sits and stares, torn from his ancient catacomb, the cold Egyptian mummy, uplifted in his coffin, at feminine admirers at Scudder's, all speechless, and dried up. His reins are on the grass, his hands hang at his side, his eyes are dimmed and dark, his mouth is stretched wide open, his head droops on his shoulder. Strange languor o'ercomes him, fierce weakness consumes him,—he wishes he was in Hell.

THE ABDUCTION.

Proserpine ! Proserpine ! hold ! beware ! temptation may be too tempting ! She little heeds the warning which Prudence, in her ears, whispers and urges ; but cheek, and eye, and tongue, and hand, are busy all coquetting. She gathers up her flowers, and presses them closely together, and binds them with the ends of her long flowing hair. And often, as she binds them, she looks, with half shut eye, through the meshes of her locks; and through her long, dark eyelashes, the beams of a mellow dreamy eye, fall, broken, upon Pluto. So, moonlight rays, through intertwining trees, sprinkle the leafy ground, in yellow autumn. And now she scatters them to the winds, and claps her empty hands, bending her bare white arms; and now she gathers the woodrose gay, and snatches the pale lily, and winds them with a willow wreath, and presses them, all trembling, against her leaping heart, and fawn-like, startled, flies, but archly she looks back and peals in Pluto's ear a merry laugh. Her maidens, delighted, encourage the flirtation, rejoicing in the grace and beauty of their mistress.

His majesty looked like a natural fool, while loud the echoed joy rang through the sacred grove. "I am seduced," thought he, "from principle and promise; from all my vows of single blessedness; from my course of life, and love of business! alas! I am seduced! She must go down to Erebus with me, for certain."

"Will you accept a violet, sir?" said Proserpine, O, how meekly! and curtesying with well-put-on solemnity, as she stood by the chariot, and lifting up the flower, exposed her upturned throat, and deep, full, swelling bust, to Pluto's glowing gaze. "Will you accept a violet, good sir?"

"Violate?" gasped the king of night, not knowing what he said. "Yes, yes, my angel, yes, jump in;" and Pluto's iron arm was on the maiden's cestus, and into the chariot lifted her.

Away!—away!—What voice is that, shaking the trembling air, and urging Pluto's steeds! Alas! alas! what grief is that, so long, so loud, so bitter? What goddess pleads so piteously, and who is deaf to her prayer? Ye maidens at Pergus, say, why do ye weep, beating your breasts, and tearing your hair! Where, where is your mistress?

Lost Proserpina's shrieks no gentle pity moved in her immortal ravisher. Upon his coursers' necks, abandoned, lie the reins, for both his hands are needed, the maiden's cries to stifle, and bind her active arms down, and keep her in the chariot. The steeds dash on the accustomed way, o'er hill and dale, swamp and marsh, " rocks, caves, lakes, fens, bogs, dens, and shades of death," the dreary road to Tartarus.

" Oh! mother! mother! goddess Ceres!" besought the struggling girl ; " save your unhappy daughter."

" Be quiet, love, you shall be queen of Hell, my bride, my wife," said Pluto, bending upon one knee, and still, with equal zeal, encouraging his horses, each by name ;—" To reign is worth ambition, though in Hell ; ' better to reign in Hell, than serve in Heaven,' " pursued the seducer, quoting his old friend Orpheus. " People may talk of the need of a minister, Hymen, or flamen, to sanction a match, but believe me, the doctrine's suspicious and sinister. A license to marry? It is a mere catch—it 's all in my eye—and so says Fanny Wright—nay, Proserpine, I prithee, do not cry so bitterly ; these tears fall worse than idly."

Tears, promises, and prayers, threats, flattery, and protestations—how mingled all, and all how vain! The raptured bride no consolation knew, for being made a queen against her virgin will—none but the old man's wealth and extensive dominion—what goddess or woman was ever so foolish but that she would listen to reason?

"O! what a horrid beard!" said Proserpine, quite faintly —" and then—your breath is so sulphureous,"—

"Fear not, my dearest, Saunders has just new honed my razors—* * * * *—and then your majesty may rest assured, there is no better seidlitz in the world than a good draught of Lethe."

But now they reached the realms of modest Cyane, cool, chaste, immaculate nymph; the coursers' heated hoofs hiss in her sacred fountain.   An ancient nymph was she, of puritan extraction, a rigid methodist, and censor stern of fleshly weaknesses.   Three thousand years had rolled over her virgin head, yet had no wanton lip tasted her withered cheek. Up, from the parting waves, ascended the cold nymph, and chilled the raging team with sudden frost.   The chariot stood still.

"Who bars our way?" cried the imperial lover—"and stays our happy nuptials?"

"'T is I forbid the banns," said the lady of the lake, putting her arms akimbo.   "Have you never yet heard of an action *per quod*, for running away with a woman?   By G—d!   This is too much, a veteran monarch like you, not waiting to ask for permission to sue, leaving old Ætna, and steering for Gretna, you, surely, are crazy, or else you are blue.   Ah! my poor girl, I pity your unhappy—"

"Pray, mind your own business, good madam," said Proserpine, sharply, but hiding her face with her hands.

The king of Orcus waited for no more, hearing with grim delight the words of spite and passion blended.   Upon the yielding earth, with fierce and violent strength, he smote his whipstock.   Straightway there lay disclosed, precipitous, but smooth, a turnpike new macadamised, leading down to the kingdom.   The adamantine gates shone dimly through the shades, in dusky brightness, and on his eager ear, glad in the welcome sound, fell the accustomed bark of trusty Cerberus. " We'll soon be home, my love."

" O ! whither do you bear me ? stay ! curb your rushing steeds !   How dark !—stay !—stay !—I faint !—the air !—release me !—in pity let me go !—let me go home to my mother !"—.

" Not to-night, Proserpine, not to-night."

" When, when, in mercy—when ?" shrieked the lost penitent.

" Never, Proserpine, never."

THE INTRODUCTION.

" Infernal world, and thou, profoundest hell,
Receive thy new possessor,"

said the happy Pluto, bowing reverentially, as he drove through the everlasting portals.   " Down Cerberus, down.   I give you welcome, Proserpine, and joy, in your new dominion—back, you bloody three mouthed cur—droop not, my gentle queen, you will soon become accustomed to the change of air—we are populous here, you see, but not crowded.   This is the Styx, and that little murmuring stream on the right, is Acheron. The people down the river to the left, are ghosts waiting to cross the ferry ; but we, you perceive, dash right ahead, through fire and water, without stopping for the boat.   Here we are in Tartarus proper.   The individuals you see engaged in different employments, are all persons of the highest consideration—I'll soon introduce you—you'll be delighted—ah ! allow me to present to you Mr. Tantalus, the president of our infernal Temperance Society—a very abstemious, self-denying gentleman—drinks nothing—Mr. Tantalus, the queen of Or-

cus—you look thirsty, sir—steady, you fiery colts—Proserpine, the Misses Danaides—daughters of a king, my dear, and
eminent collaborators with Tantalus, in the liquid cause—deep
in the science of water power—Ladies, our new queen will
give out cards for a ball, as soon as she is rested from her
journey. Lord Sysiphus, my love — a great mineralogist.
Hippodamia, we must tax thy dutiful loyalty to set down that
water pitcher, and do us a few errands. Let our people hear
the news, and share their sovereign's joy. First see chief justice Minos, and desire him to hasten to the palace to draw a
marriage settlement—carry Mr. Tantalus a bottle of hock—
tell him, I say he *must* drink it—set Ixion's wheel turning the
other way—drive the vultures from off old Tityus, and tell all
the souls to rest themselves and be happy ; this is our royal
wedding-day, and our bridal shall be a jubilee, by the Styx !

Smack, went the whip, and on dashed the royal vehicle,
burning the tracks of its rapid course in lines of vivid lightning.

THE SUBMISSION.

Within an iron chamber, deep in the sombre palace, were
crouching three old women, sitting and spinning, sad, solemn,
sullen, sulky, scandalous. The threads those women spun,
were of no earthly texture ; the hands that held that distaff,
were of no terrene mould, no mortal fingers they that shut
those bright edged scissors, opened and shut, and cut the
fated thread of human life. Mournfully, mysteriously, went
round your magic wheel, ye priestesses of Destiny, when Hell
received your mistress, rival, and queen. Why should gan-
grenous jealousy corrupt the eternal Parcæ ? Why pales their
sinking cheek, why fades their ancient eye, why falls their

thin red hair, all matted on their bony necks, reeking with proofs of recent lack of combs, and clean rain water!

Proserpine sleeps on Pluto's neck, and Erebus rejoices. Now haste, the bridal bed bedeck, ye ghosts lift up your voices; fill high with vinum Samium, and swell the glad Epithalamium.

High on a throne, which carpenters far famed, on earth, of yore, but now mechanic ghosts, had temporary raised upon a hill, covered with carpets, Brussels and Ingrain, Pluto exalted sat; by twelve steps raised to that good eminence; and, from his seat, the summoned myriads of his realm surveyed, Tartarean and Elysian. By his side, queenly, his bride sat wondering at the shades, jostling, and for good places eager pressing. As, when from senior's pews, the silken gowned step glorious, and o'erspread the covered stage, on glad commencement-day—day of relief from board with circles chalked, and conic sections—solemn, grave Præses sits, and Latin talks, and morals; in the body of the church, sound fans incessant, beating the hot air; while youth, ingenuous, plies the elbow.

The monarch, by the sight uplifted, slowly rose, and murmuring plaudits rumbled through the crowd as he began to speak. "Spirits and ghosts, our subjects dutiful"—but here, a sudden clap of interposing thunder stopped the begun infliction, announcing unexpectedly, a messenger from Jove. Mercury knelt at the feet of the king, and handed him a letter.

Pale Proserpine trembled, while Pluto, muttering, broke the seal, and swore, in a low tone—and loud Alecto laughed, shaking her tied up snakes,—tied with white ribbons, for the bridal—as o'er his royal shoulder, bending joyous, she read the following epistle.

" Dear Plute,

"This a cursed bad business of yours about Proserpine. Ceres is raising the very Old Nick, up here, and we shall have no quiet until you let the girl go. I have had to promise the old woman, that if her daughter has not eaten, since you have had her,——you know what that means—you shall give her up entirely, but if she has tasted food on your premises, that——then——then she shall divide her time, half yearly, between you and her mother. Come, now, that's an equitable decision—don't appeal, you shall have the first six months, my boy——

Thy affectionate brother,

JOVE OMNIP."

"P. S. Send me a box of good pocket matches—I'm quite out—how are you off for nectar ? J."

" She has eaten, she has eaten," blabbed mean Ascalaphus, young grey-eyed imp, delighted at the chance to do his master service. " She has eaten, she has eaten, within the Elysian fields ; in the shadow of an arbor I was sitting, when the queen, on her tiptoe stretching up, plucked a nectarine, and ate it !"

Another peal of thunder ! The snakes upon the heads of the furies hissed and grinned, and Mercury flew back to heaven.

CLASSIC RHAPSODIES.

NO. II.

A ROMAN CHARIOT RACE.

BY M. T. CICERO.

To the Spirit of the Turf and Soul of the Times.

I SEND the enclosed with an apology for not translating ALL the Latin. My plea is, that some friend has miscellaneously borrowed my dictionary. Don't expect, however, to be troubled again, in this way, for I have written to Tully that he has more time to study the people's American than I have to figure out the Consul's Latin, and that the next chapter be all in our vernacular.*   Yours respectfully,

J. CYPRESS, Jr.

* That is rather a lame excuse for a man who means to trot fair. What is it but saying " my groom left the stable door open and somebody stole my saddle ?"—But what can WE do ? will some of the legal branches of our tree of knowledge let a small apple of advice fall into our lap ? Seven and sixpence we paid to a night-school-teacher to dig into one of our ministerial imps, how to render an account current of the stuff into our vernacular. We forbear to do more than to add the render—the get. Here it is !
" Cicero in Elysium—heathen E—next door to—vide Virgil :—
 Taking his comfort,
                                            " To
 Porter, of all joys the gentle guardian,—
 Times chronicler, magnificent and Spirit dear :—
 Court, Chief, of Wagner and Old Whitenose, Justice of,
 Master of horse, head Register of Turf,
 And Jove knows what else not— *   *   *   *
 —Taking the shine off every common chariot—
 With such a drive—
 L. L. D.—O. K., &c. &c. &c.
         " Respectfully and profoundly,
            " With sentiments of the highest consideration,
               " Have the honor to be, &c.

Cicero, in Elysio, jucunditatem imbibens,
    Portero, gaudiorum janitori
    Temporum spiritui, magnifico, carissimo,
    Stadiorum, Wagnerorum, Bostonium, gubernatori,
    Equitum omnium magistro registroque
    Splendorem abstrahenti omnibus loaferibus ordinariis
    L. L. D.———O. K.———&c. &c. &c.
                                    Salutcm.

Quantum dolorem acceperim, et quanto fructu sim privatus et forensi et domestico,—Cato and Socrates who room with me take on dreadfully about it,—Aquilæ canœ ab illa dirutione infelicissimâ, tertio cursu, te prœsente flenteque, besides the burst up of the match between Wagner and Boston, and old Eclipse colting on his former laurels as though he was stadii functus officio ;—and not a heroic stallion to adjure by, on the course, imprimis, pro nostra consuetudine existimare potes. Next, all that I have to say, is, that I send you an account of an old race that was run a little way out of town when I practised law in Rome. It was just before Cataline abused my patience so that I had to kick him out of the house. Sceleratus ! Snakes ! Infernissimus ! Fire and tow ! Inter infernos ! I won seven thousand Aurei Denarii—none of your patent

"How much grief I have been cursed with, and how much enjoyment I have been deprived of, both domestic and forensic"—then comes some English—after that—"by that infernal break down of Grey Eagle on the third heat, you being present and weeping—more Latin—'stadii functus officio'—used up—then a little more English, to the word 'course' inclusive, then, in the first place read · imprimis'—which every body knows by heart :—go on—'according to our fashion, my dear fellow.' The rest is easy as losing a bet. Do you want to go on any thing privately ? Put up your currency. The dew will rust it. Peace, the swifest kind of horses —a Westly Richards fowling piece of the last and most ample build, rod and hooks lucky, and most of all a mistress true and beautiful be with you."
That's pretty much the story. The note is rather familiar than modest. But, as we said before, what *can* we do ? Cicero writes, and we can't lose a word of the letter. We shall call our next colt "*Atticus*," after ourselves.—Editors.

shinplasters—from him upon that race, and the false wretch refused to fork up. [Between you and me, that was the reason I came down upon him in that " *Quosque-TANDEM*" style so fulguriously. ⁻I rather used him up there. If Pluto will let him come out, I'll go the same team against him again. But he must plank the cash.] *Pignus deponere*, and then back out or forget the name of the horse you bet on, and refuse to let the stake-holder pay over—that's almost as bad as going—through a friend—against your own nag—call him—Deafaway—and hammering a tack into his hip bone on the morning he is to start, and swearing at your trainer for letting the nails fall out of his shoes upon the stable floor. Pax, equi perceleririssimi, Westlei Ricardi ultimœ amplisimœque structuræ bombarda, arundo, hami que fausti, et, maxime, amica sincera et alma, tecum.

P.S. I have enclosed the documents, I speak of, to my friend, J. Cypress, Jr., to translate for you. He knows my " p's" and " q's," and I don't want my hand to get familiar with your devils.

P.P.S. Your Spirit comes here very irregularly. I wish you would write a letter to the C. and Enquirer, and blow up Amos Kendall, that Loco Foco postmaster. Pretty loco—not to know better *our locus* in quo. If existing contracts go on much more, I shall abandon all hopes of your ever getting a permanent foothold on Elysian Turf.* Cato sends his best respects. If you see Colonel Johnson, tell him I've got a new white hat that I want to bet on against any *trifle* that he will *run* against its *fly* in a thunder-squall. Why don't he bring out something? Are American horses good for nothing but to make smoked beef for soldiers in Florida?—Pax, again, tecum, et tuo Spiritu. Sing now this.

* Amos has since resigned.—ED.

2*

PSALMODIC SERVICE.

Air—" Nonne vides ?"

" Hast thou beheld, when from the goal they start,
The youthful charioteers with beating heart
Rush to the race ; and panting scarcely bear
Th' extremes of feverish hope, and chilling fear ;
Stoop to the reins, and lash with all their force ;
The flying chariot kindling in its course.
And now alow and now aloft they fly,
As borne thro' air, and seem to touch the sky ;
No stop ; no stay ; but clouds of dust arise
Spurned and cast backward on the followers' eyes ;
The hindmost blows the foam upon the first.
Such is the love of praise, and honorable thirst."

THE LUPERCAL WAS PAST. The solemn priests, with ves-
tals bearing torches—fed from the flame that burned young
Romulus a king, swift rushing from a lupine mother—
majestic, paced the stones of Rome, that sang beneath their
glad retiracy, and, thirsty, sought the secret places of their
temples. " We've had enough of such revivals," now quoth
youthful Curtius, descendant he direct—so his blood showed
forth, rich swelling in his neck veins—from him who leaped
his horse into that horrid gulf to save his country, filling the
gaping ditch, not with his body juvenile, but with his glowing
soul. Deep from his mother's breast, and pure, he sucked the
essence of the noble soul of daring Scævola. Mutius she called
him, as she staunched the crimson glory of his severed arm, the
hand cut off to throw into the teeth of a besieger of the walls
that held his Love.

Mount Palatine, Tarpeian Hill, Curia Hostilia, Esquiline
Place, Aventine Row, Viminal Square, and all the other building lots laid out for private use at public expense, from Battery to Tauri Caput, ejected their eye-rubbing sun-rivals.

Apollo laid the string on, and whipped his steamy dawn-dancers into foam, so that he might see the race, and hold back Sol at least two heats, and then have time to cool an easy jog by nightfall, and light fierce Peleus down to the barnacled bedchamber of expecting Thetis.

"Forum boarium"—Fly-market,—"Forum piscarium"—Catharine-slip,—all punctured mutton, and flounders fast decaying—smiling in death, like Patience on a monument, in hope long lingering, for a Five-point bidder—threw out their tainted stock, and in the dock most merciful, full fed the doubtful eels. No proud Basilica contained a solitary dandy, in a new coat unpaid for, strutting. No safe Comitium, with threatened vengeance of "contempt of court," held a pert lawyer, boring the sick Subsellia. No Rostrum breasted out the figure-head of orators. No bullock died, no dove was sacrificed with riteful ceremonies. The fanes, altars, temples all, and theatres were silent. The sacred groves let loose their grasshoppers. Glad pedagogues discharged their scholars alphabetic, and horse-hide flogged, in extacies, preferred to joy of human flesh-cuts. Plebeians, patrons, orators, patricians, knights, poets, freedmen, loafers, and logicians, homeborn, Gallician, British slaves, and Afric—the city Prætor, the newly appointed sub-treasury Quæstor, the tribunes of "the people"—office seekers—and of the seven-hilled tyrant every scrub shoemaker was afoot, and for the stadium panting. It was a race-day, and notes were not protested. Every body rose before daylight to be happy. Two *capiases* only were issued to the Sheriff during twenty-four hours. Both of these, however, were in actions on the case for felonious insinuation by German *liberti* in paying bills of a fraudulent banking incorporation, which Cataline had *dinnered and suppered and drunk* through the Senate—for the amount of their by-bets as to who would take the lead. They were held to bail. I would rather be a bale of cotton, and walked over by all the niggers in Louisiana, than to be handled and footed as they were after the go was done—

> " On sharp-cut rails their ragged corduroy sat,
> The conscious chesnut smoking with their fat."

The ladies' stand was gemmed with pearls and brilliants, early. Brightly Metella sparkled, lip-love full. Gently, with languid goodness, fainting, repulsing, seemingly, with half-forgiving, half-inviting eye-lashes, that fanned the air into a poisonous deliciousness of agony, as it blew death of Love, and love of Death, upon the unaccustomed eye-ball of the long-locked, yellow-curled Ascanius in the next box—who dared to bet a pair of gloves against her—sat, shone, killed—O! sweetest murder!—the terrible Lucretia ;—omnipotent in Beauty, cruel Victress! gentle Tyrant! merciless happiness! wearing Grief in one pitying ear, Heaven haughty in the other !—rings—rings—Lorenzo ;—everlasting circles of mad idolatry, half hidden by careless tresses ;—no other jewel showing but a breast-bound ruby, that swelled out upon her partly—by accident—unkerchiefed bosom, in the excitement of the race ;—nothing much—a strawberry—a rosebud. Proud was the eye that on *her* bust might look and blench not. *He* might gaze into the sun by summer noonday—Eagle challenger. Such was a *Roman's* daughter—Woman and Goddess mixed. Is the blood all lost ? Are there no Deities whom we of modern years may love and worship too. Is it all ——*

The eternal city gasped with hot anxiety. Not a newspaper was published on that morn, except the " Bona Dea Ob-

---

* I can't make this sentence out ; Cicero must come up and explain himself.—J. C. Jr.

server." The ode to Hiero, done into smooth Iambics by the club laureate, was in the mouths of all, excluding thoughts of trade in sugar and tobacco.* The *laticlavium* ruffled its broad

* Pindar, the best poet in the world—whom Horace calls "inimitable"—wrote his poems in praise of swift horses, and victorious riders. Hiero was a king, and a gentleman,-but he was not too proud to ride his own matches. The first Olympic is addressed to him as a horseback-man, the second to him as a charioteer. Quinctilian goes the craziest nonsense about the Poet's Union—Olympic—Beacon—Pythian—Camden—Nemean—and Trenton—Isthmian—course outpourings. Some of them are fair, that's a fact. But I can't find the time set down in a single report. Time, or no time, however, it would make some of our nags grit their teeth, to read the odes in the original Greek.

One principal reason why our turf is so quiet, so deathlike, is that the club don't elect a poet laureate, and people are ashamed, or dare not, mount their own steeds.—The only exceptions are in the cases of an English steeple-chase, and an Irish fox-hunt.—Let somebody come out with something in the style of

" Quadrupedante putrem sonitu quatit ungula campum"

and the very dust upon the track will turn into India Rubber, and pitch the horses onward, as though Burns' witches were after them. Then, then we might be able to come home and say

"There was mounting 'mong boys of the Netherby clan

Fosters, Fenwicks, and Musgraves, they rode and they ran ;"

and remember how bright and brave was the gallant cavalier who so gracefully reined back his curving charger, before the admiring ladies. up to taw, in front of the Judges' Stand. Now, instead of a chivalrous knight willing to do to death for the cross that hangs upon his ladye-love's forehead, we look upon the ghastly face of some pale boy, consumptive, blanket-sweated, to bring him down to weight ; or upon the black *eye*-vory, and the white ivory of an Abyssinian baboon licked into the shape of humanity, and pivotted with tiny feet upon the back of a steed who neighs for a master. What pretty execution would that babe do against helmet, cuirass and slashing battle-axe ! Knighthood ! horsemanship ! Bring up your horses ! That's a good cry, and enables one to say a thing or two in favor of modern racing. It sounds like that " *Quadrupedante*" sentence I just now quoted from Virgil. I heard it when Eclipse lost the first heat, and *a man* mounted him. I knew that Purdy would win. I saw his eye. It was like a conqueror's. I saw his seat. It was firm as Roman cement ten years old. He was glued to the saddle. He was part of the horse. I saw a centaur that once. His legs added two ribs to the glorious steed, but were adopted and formed a happy strengthening plaster to the whole family circle. His left hand felt the bit, and Eclipse looked back. His eyes, at a glance, told him there was no mistake about that feel. Then there walked up to the starting post, a dignified, fleet, and certain nag, as ever retrieved begun defeat, folds alongside the humble *angusti* work of sixpenny tailors. The *Plebs communis*, and the *Turba sine nomine* of sleepers under stoops, communed with senators and knights, and eased nobility of quickly bagged sestertia, by honest thimble-riggery. Jove! how full the air and roads were! Bacchus turned out his tigers before a pearl-silvered wagonett, built by Opifex & Co., out of a monster oyster-shell, fresh captured from the Lucrine lake. Not a horse was left in Rome. The lady Abbess of the Convent of the Delphic oracle, drove, four-in-hand, a team of wild-cats. Mercury lit upon an oak that overlooked the course. Iris got up a shower and sat upon a rainbow. Vulcan smuggled himself inside the track, under pretence that he was a blacksmith, sent to shoe a colt who had lost his slipper. Mars was seen fighting an Irishman, who had got drunk on bad liquor. Ceres stretched up her auburn flowing tresses in a neighboring corn-field on the hill-side. Pan was pointing out the nags to her. All—aye, all—were there ; Gods, Mortals, and Infernals. Happy, happy Rome ! sole city worthy of such glorious company !

bearing upon his back one whom we might have wished to have lived in Pindar's time, but for the hope he will yet contrive to bring the Sun and Moon together, get up a new Eclipse, and ride a triumph again.—*Printer's Asmodeus.*

CHAPTER II.

————" palmaque nobilis
Terrarum dominos evehit ad Deos."—HORACE, Ode 1.

" Few people ritely estimate the furious luxuriaunce of an old fashioned
Romanne Course. Pitie 'tis, no Turffe Registrar chronicled the glorious
height of heates of those braue ages. Saue only the poetts did record
" evehit ad Deos," or some suche loose reporte. Time, pedigree, endu-
raunce, speede, be mostlie lost. Muche 'tis to be feared the begarlie
Monkes who should haue been burned wh hotte fire, haue erasede out
manie choice accomptes from the parchmente scroules of the triumphs at
the Campus Martius, whereon to rite their stupide missals, and haue little
lefte behinde saue imperfecte legendes. Yet euen from wolves, the halfe
eaten lambe torne, wh violent force uppone their gnashing teeth dothe to
the hungrie exploarer of antique fatherre-lands taste like manna to a wandering sinnere of Israel in the wilderness. Soe to a trew louer of a good
horse raice dothe fashion forthe for ituself a noble grace an aunciente char-
riott struggle, albeit Monkish Latinne roll between, being, so to speeke,
the axle of the wheels."—WINK : ed. 1649, p. 46.

IT was no common meeting. The sporting world of Rome,
and all its provinces, were on the Campus Martius. Spain
sent her jennets from her dark Moriscan stables, and her wild
mountain rovers flashed their long manes around the heads of
their safe-seated Guerillas. Gaul entered untrimmed fetlocks.
Brittania stamped the track with heavy cart-horse hoofs. Sar-
matia sweated, Dacia pránced upon the track. Greece stood
unsaddled in clear Spartan ribs, and trod, beside this simple
fit-out, magnificent in rich Corinthian adornment. Numidia
sent her wild eye-lightnings, and Libya tramped the plain with
foaming teeth. Egypt entered Cleopatra,—Black Maria of
her mistress queen. Syrian, Babylonian, Median, Mesopota-
mian, all, were there. Felix Arabia walked out her splendid
stallions, bitted by stately Bedouins. The Imaum of Muscat
glorified his country by the challenge of two lippers of the
Persian Gulf. Great Jupiter ! what an anniversary !

The Course was free for all four-year-olds that never had

been matched before ; chariots not be more than four feet from hub to hub of hind wheel ; steeds unlimited in number,—the parties litigant to draw for places.

The Prætor's trumpet blew a summon blast, and straight a host of pawing combatants neighed at the starting post. The *Meta* was scarcely seen for feather floaters. The Red, the White, the Green, the Blue, the Golden and the Purple mountings mingled sparklings of ambition for the glory of success.* It was a goodly sight to see the foamy rush of the wave-breasted steeds stopped on the instant into marble statue movement by the stern muscles of their godlike drivers. First stood Marcellus, with his followers in *Blue*, holding a pair of milk-white colts from Elis, unbroken yet, but kind, great in their name, the gift of a Greek girl, daughter of a happy hero who bore away the wreath victorious at the last Olympic, and died as he was crowned. 'T was said their sires were the horses of the Sun, who in the last eclipse stole time and loved their vein-swollen mothers. Hard upon him pressing, scarcely, with desperate force, young Julius reined his four-in-hand of dark-lashed Gypsies—true bred, fresh, fed with grain, and groomed upon the meadows of the Nile, and signalled by their nature, *Green*. Whose panting ardor steamed by his side ? 'T was Sergius Cataline sending fire through his reins to the fifth couple-leaders.† Close by his side rushed all his band of friends, traitors to Rome—pimps of intriguing Fulvia, rob-

* The four ancient companies were the *Prasina*, the *Russata*, the *Alba* or *Albata*, and the *Veneta ;* the Green, the Red, the White, the Sea Colored or Sky Colored. This distinction was taken from the color of their liveries. * * * Domitian added two new companies, the Golden and the Purple."—KENNETT, R. A.

† "In ordinary reading we meet only with the *Bigæ* and the *Quadrigæ ;* but they sometimes had their *Sejuges*, *Septemjuges*, &c. Suetonius assures us that when Nero was a performer in the Olympic game, he made use of a ' Decemjugis,' or chariot drawn with ten horses together."—Ib.

bers of virtuous youth, and haters fierce of keen watching Cicero. Cassius and Cethegus, Lentulus and Curius, stood each—in false conspiracy, urging ferocious warrior steeds to aid their leader, and defeat the faction upon which Cicero had bet with Cataline—in chariots side-armed with scythes, to cut their adversaries' horses down. They flared in *Red*. Next stood Gracchus, proud in his gorgeous family "*Purple*." Mark Antony shone in *Gold* behind six proud-necked bit-champers. Last of all, a Knight, unknown, stood like a god, with foot advanced upon his dashboard of pure pearl, grooming, with skilful ease, three pair of coal-black ear-glistening limb-tremblers, unable to stand still, and rolling fire from their nostrils,*—himself and reins and harness all in brilliant white, and sparkling steel. The ladies cried "behold Apollo!" as they owned with beating hearts the heavenly grace of his recognition of the shouts of commendation which went to the skies from the hundred thousand throats ;† and freely wagered rings and bracelets upon the gallant stranger's triumph.

The sacred rites were celebrated, the lots were drawn, and straight, obedient to the rules established, the factions took their stations. The Master of the Lude dropped his white

---

* "Stare loco nescit, micat auribus, et tremit artus,
Collectumque premens volvit sub maribus ignem."
VIRG. GEORGIOS.

† "There were several of these Circi in Rome. The most remarkable was Circus Maximus, first built by Tarquin. The length of it was four stadia, or furlongs, the breadth the like number of acres, with a trench of ten foot deep, and as many broad, to receive the water ; and seats enough for one hundred and fifty thousand men. It was extremely adorned and beautified by succeeding princes, particularly by Julius Cæsar, Augustus, &c., and enlarged to such an extent as to be able to contain in their proper seats, two hundred and sixty thousand spectators."—KENNETT.

"Some moderns say 380,000. Its circumference was a mile."—ADAMS ROM. ANTIQ.

MEM.—Kennett and Adams differ in their way and result of estimation of length and breath.—

kerchief, and then dashed, with ocean-like ferocity, the rainbow-painted waves of the raging combatants. Julius took the lead, and " Green !" " Green !" was the cry. Hard behind lashed Cataline, and all his faction. " Blue," " purple," " white," and " golden," seemed to hang back to watch the chance for a dash.

" Green !—Blue !—Purple !—Golden !" went up the shouts from the friends of the different factions as they became involved in dust, and locked each other's wheels. None cried " Red," for even the stable boys hated Cataline. " White !" screamed Lucretia, although he lagged behind, and seemed to fear. " White against the field."

" You are a fool," said Mrs. Cornelius Grab-us Agrip-onus, who sat near her.

" The chiel's distraught," quietly remarked an old Scotch servant-woman behind,—brought out by the Cæsar,—" what'll ye bet, my lassie ?"

The baby which the slave had on her arm then set up a domestic yell, and with the vociferations of the boy, and people in the box—" I want to go home"—and " Turn her out"—Lucretia's answer was lost. What cared she ?

" The White !—look !"—shouted Lucretia ; " see ! he is discounting lashes freely ! His whip touches the flank of the near side leader ! He is in the melee ! He gains ! He is ahead of all but Cataline !"

" I can't see, my dear, so plain as thee can," said an African Quakeress, whom the Spirit had moved to come from the borders of the Red Sea to see this uncommon race,—" I can't see, my dear, so well as thee, on account of the dust, but I think, I mean, I fear thee is in love with that ' White,'—his mistress, likely,—but he'll burst his boiler, and smash his bank—chariot I mean—before he gets to the first Meta."

"Out on thee! for a foul witch!" replied Lucretia, very quietly,—like all women,—and, suiting the action to the word, laid, with impressive significance, the back of her hand upon the fat lips of the prophetic Abyssinian. Faintness followed, and the doorkeeper, with the utmost kindness, dragged out the smitten slave. She never attended quaker meetings again. Drs. Auger and Aruspex, and their students, dug her up about a year afterwards, and one of them delivered a lecture over her bones at the Museum on the interesting topic of Ourang Outangs.

"White! white! white!" now vociferated the excited girl. But none would bet her more, and the timid began to hedge— hard work, too, to find a hedge to hide behind—for the noble lady's shouts had reached the unknown's ear, and he was mad with strength and skill.

Short time was there to bet or hedge; for the first meta[*] was approached by such a troop of sweepstakers as never had been seen before. Some honor-seeker *must* be dashed against the horrid columns, dedicated to the gods, which marked the turning point, or crushed between the antagonistic chariots. Who must be thrown under prostrate horses! Who must die? "On, white;" cried Cicero. "Whip, golden!"— "Whip, green!" halloed some shoemaker's apprentices, and laborers of *Erinnys*. "Steady, hold! White! white! for the love of Heaven! hold and wait!" shrieked Lucretia. Mark, mark, how impious Cataline and his crew let out their

---

[*] "There was at the one end of the cirque certaine barriers, *id est* places barred or railed in, at which place the horses began the race; and at the other end was the marke, whether the horses ran : it was called in Latin *Meta*, and the barriers *Carceres, a coercendo*. Whence we say ' *a Carceribus ad Metam*,' that is, from the beginning to the ending."—CRIPP's Roman Anthology, "*printed by Iohn Litchfield, Printer to the famous Vniversity, at Oxford, Ann. Dom. 1631.*"

secret-spring-bowie-scythes, and hold hard back to cut the horses of Marcellus ! The noble youth had seen, and reining hard, held back, and knew with horror, but determined vengeance, Marcellus, cut in twain, his horses madly running with half his body bleeding in his chariot. Upon the other half, prone in the dust, crowned with rich auburn locks, and eyes beautiful in death, the leaders of Mark Antony stumbled and stopped. The cursed scythe of Lentulus cut his wheel-horses. Cethegus, with his hubs of heavy steel, crushed in his chariot sides, and Mark was tossed at least full fifty yards, into the stall of an old woman who sold crabs, just outside the track. " There's an end of that poor nigger," sang out Cataline. The " Green,"—unhappy Julius, green enough,—ran against the marble column on the left, and smashed himself into life eternal. Cethegus and Lentulus pressing on, got entangled in their own snares, and cut each other. Off their nags jumped, and struck their comrade Curius. It was *curious* indeed to see how they leaped the barriers, and ran across the field. The " Gracchus" then made a bold dash, but his unwilling mare shyed, backed, and kicked at the sight of the mixed up blood of dying men and horses, and whip nor spur would make them move. None then remained but Cataline and the unknown white knight. O ! with what an agony of anxiety did Lucretia cry, " Be wary of his cursed poisonous sword-point !" " Kill him !" cried the master of the Lude— " he rides foul, and murders !" " Kill him ;"—"Stab him ;" cried the whole assembled multitude. The white knight raised his whip,—with one end he lashed his streaming leaders,—with the other, heavy loaded, he gave Mr. Cataline a crack on the head, that tumbled him out of his vehicle. His horses ran away just where they had a mind to. He fell into the trench. Some Irishmen pulled him out, but he was very muddy. Some thought he was a little drunk. The white knight walked his horses over the course, as the waves walked over the smitten Egyptians, treading upon the bodies of his foes, and took the wreath of glory.

That night he married Lucretia.

The White Knight was *the son of Cicero.*

3*

CLASSIC RHAPSODIES.

NO. III.

SUBTERRANEAN NEWS.

DEAR EDITOR,—I was reading the fifth book of the Æneid one afternoon last week, after dining magnificently upon roast pig and green peas, when, almost imperceptibly, and with a sensation of gradual, languid, pleasant metamorphosis, I was, in the body, taken out of the body, and transported to the un-monopolized public lands of poetry and classic story. Animal magnetism carried me over the track we flew. Cumœa received me, ambitious pilgrim, seeking safe convoy and a pass-port for travel through the interesting regions that own Pluto for their king. I stood upon the margin of the sacred grove, where grows the golden tree, whose branches are at once the protection-papers and the pilot of the specially favored living, to the country of ghosts and infernal gods. Mighty enterprise, glorious riches of glowing incidents! What subterranean treasures shall I glorify to the wondering upper air, if ever I get back! "Pencillings by the way"—"Crayon Sketches"—Trolloping "inklings" of a jaunt through Tartarus during the year 1839. Shade of Æneas, help me to break through these cat-briars and blackberry bushes, that guard the entrance to the sacred tree!

With this invocation I pressed boldly into the penetralia of the wood. I readily discovered the individual who keeps watch over the aureal vegetable, and expressed to her my de-sire to go to Hell. My request was received with courtesy, and the trusty watch-woman accompanied her acknowledgment of my right to prosecute the jaunt by breaking off and putting into my hand a sister branch of the bough which marshalled the pious son of Anchises some thousand years ago. I felt the god running through my veins as I touched the scion of the tree of knowledge and power.

"I presume, sir, I need not show you the way," said the civil sybil; "you New-Yorkers are generally familiar with the road; but if you should miss your track, the rod will direct you. Follow the rod. The gold will keep you straight."

I touched my hat to the old lady in acknowledgment of the complimentary observation which she was pleased to express touching my fellow-citizens, and bidding her good day, turned to commence my journey.

Immediately the under-brush and matted trees fell apart, disclosing a broad avenue of spiral green sward running down into the earth at about an angle of thirty-two and a half degrees. Down this declivity I walked, or rather was whirled by a vehement power of centripetal locomotion, which soon brought me to the boundary of the dusky empire. High, higher than sight; far—farther than thought, stretched the everlasting walls. Gloomily and fearfully the grand portals frowned before me. The gates were swung wide open, but old Cerberus was wide awake, and his three heads were busily occupied in fighting a family quarrel in reference to a bone which each appeared desirous to appropriate.

The moment he noticed me he saluted me with an ululatory recognition, which made me somewhat doubt the sufficiency of my nerves for the journey I had undertaken. I trembled more especially, because in the hurry of my setting out I had neglected to bring with me the customary *viaticum* to grease and bribe his jaws. Moreover, one does not like to strike a gentleman's dog, particularly when he is on a visit to him,

and unless the brute exhibits decided symptoms of hydropho-
bia. But the impetus of my progress was such, that there
was no time for adjustment of the difficulty. " I must settle
this business with Pluto," said I to myself. Then I took
courage and thought of Hercules, who dragged the cur to
earth and back again ; and raising my metal, no lightly-loaded
weapon, I got in readiness—a blow at the rushing whelp,
which, if it had been discharged in the proper direction, would
have probably made him a constellation alongside of his brother
Sirius. But, oh! wonder-working gold ! the moment that the
treasure glittered in his eyes, the three-mouthed coward fawned
and grovelled at my feet, kissing the yellow rod, like a skin-
ner before a money-lender at a quarter before three.

" Charge ! good dog," said I, patting his heads successively,
to make sure of his good opinion when I should return ; and
under these established terms of friendship, we separated. I
soon arrived at the east bank of the Styx, where I found innumerable ghosts, walking up and down, and waiting their
turn to cross. The throng at this landing place reminded me
of the congregation at the Brooklyn ferry on a race day ; only
the people were all on foot. My magic passport gained me
an easy opening through the multitude, most of whom seemed
to be Ethiopians and low Irish. Those who held themselves
more respectable stood back at a distance from the river, and
a few groups that I particularly noticed, appeared by their ges-
tures, and the occasional emphatic words which sruck my ear,
to be discussing some question about the monopoly of the
ferry. The doctrine of equal rights, however, was faithfully
regarded. No exclusive facilities for entering into the kingdom were allowed. Every candidate was duly billeted, the
moment he arrived by the constables of the vestibule, and each
took turn according to the number of his ticket, without any

inquiry made as to property, citizenship, or naturalization : all that was required was the paying for his ferriage. When I arrived at the brink of the sluggish stream, the ferryman had just put out with a cargo of small children. But on the instant he caught a glimpse of the golden rod, he returned and hurried out his passengers with fierce precipitation, forgetting, in his haste, to pay back the ferriage he had received.

"Step in, step in, step in. Welcome to Erebus. Don't see flesh and blood every day. Give us your fist. Where do you hail from ? Allow me to inhale once again the fragrance of that——snuff, snuff—my soul ! Over ! Ov—a—re—no, I beg your pardon, sir. You shall not be annoyed with any of the greasy ghosts. A mere slip of the tongue—my calling. I'll row you over alone with pleasure."

I gave the hand of the veteran mariner a hearty grasp, and at his beckoning, took a seat in the stern-sheets, and off he put.

We had hardly got six yards from the bank, when a familiar voice, a little way down the stream, assailed my ears with a loud hilloa. I turned at the cry, and to my utter astonishment, saw my old friend Jack Furnace, who had sailed only ten days before for Liverpool, in perfect health, swinging his hands above his head, and shouting.

"Mercy ! protect us !" cried I. "Jack, is that you ? Charon, my dear boy, shove back and take him in."

"That's contrary to law," replied the old gentleman. "Don't you see his ticket is numbered 11,251,956 ? There's a whole army to cross before he can tread my plank."

"You will most particularly oblige me, my esteemed friend, if you will, in this single instance, suspend the operation of the provisions of your charter. That gentleman, whose demise I am thus suddenly called on to deplore, owes me a very convenient thousand on the result of a discussion at brag. a fortnight since, and I should be happy to get his order upon his executors or administrators, to pay the amount to me out of his assets. Poor Jack! What could have killed him? Indeed, dear Charon, you must take him in. Allow me to present to you this twig of my bough, as a trifling token of my regard to your friendship, and the firmness of your adherence to the established usages of your boat."

" Don't mention this on the other side," said the old man, thrusting the argument into his pantaloons' pocket, with some rapidity ; at the same time bending and pretending to fix a thole-pin and backing water. "Old Minos would have me indicted, if he were to find out that in a single case bribery and corruption had made me lose sight of the equal rights of the ghosts. I should certainly be turned out of office."

Jack jumped in about mid-ship, and, ghost as he was, nearly swamped the ricketty craft with his irregular weight. He was fat, puffed, and, strange for a shade, red-faced, and worse and worse, was evidently inebriated. His marvellous appearance excited very natural inquiry. His story was soon told. He and the captain, crew, and passengers of the vessel he had sailed in, had just got down from the bed of the Atlantic Ocean. On the tenth day out at 4 A.M. sea time, they ran upon a mountain of ice floating under water, and in five minutes after, in a brisk flaw, foundered and went to the bottom. Jack was at his wine at the time, when he was quite as unpleasantly as unexpectedly called upon to change his liquor. Jack's inclination always did use to be in favor of drinking many bumpers rather than to submit to a single glass of brine. I could not, therefore, help saying to him, that it must have been rather mortifying to be subjected to the punishment imposed upon people who want to keep sober, while he was giving unchallengable evidence of his determination to get drunk. My suggestion did not seem to find favor with my—now—fellow-passenger, and former fellow-sinner.

"No *post mortem* reflections, Jerry," said Jack, mournfully; "you're not Coroner—it's a bad business—bad—bad. I'm very penitent. Cut off in my prime—no notice to quit—unhouselled—unanointed!—What killed you my boy?"

"I'm not dead, Jack; I'm on a voyage of discovery—playing Orpheus. Though I don't mean to pick up a wife here. By-the-by—do you remember that thousand? Can't you give me an order on your executors?"

"No money, Jerry—no money. Bursted. I'll give you a deed, when we get across, for my New Brighton speculation, and my City Lots in Kimakewahamaya. Have you got such a thing as an obolus about you, to pay this old cock? what's that? Gold! by Jove! I haven't seen such a piece of bullion for—" And here my dear friend sprang up and dashed at my magic branch.

"Sit down—sit down—you'll upset us—you'll be overboard;" cried our oarsman. But the caution came too late. Our whiffling skiff shivered quick from larboard to starboard, dipping her gunnels into the water, and Jack lost his feet, and then there was a splash, and the waters of the Styx closed over the head of my unfortunate debtor.

"There he goes. Served him right. Just as I expected," remarked the philosophic boatman, as he kept pulling on.

"Stop! stop! Charon, back water! the man will be drowned!"

"Drowned, will he? He was drowned this morning. That's three kinds of liquor he's been in to-day;" and the grim ferryman grinned.

" But he has n't secured my debt, what will become of him ?"

" Go to the bottom, to be sure. Here's where I generally lose such fellows. Just half way from shore. Call it ' half seas over hole.' Grand place for eels."

" But my venerable Remex, consider my deep interest in his fate.——Consider my thousand dollars. Can't you get him up ? How deep is it ?"

" Never went down to see. Don't fret. He can't exundize for as many years as he owes you dollars. When the time comes, he'll float ashore t'other side, and take his trial with the ghosts of people who have never been buried. Don't you know it 's the law that people that an't buried can't cross the Styx for a thousand years ?"

I remembered the statute as quoted by divers of the poets, and yielded to the necessity of its requisitions.

Seeing me melancholy, the old man lit up a good-natured smile.——" Come, cheer up," said he, " cheer up. What's the news on earth ? How do parties get on in America ? Glorious country, that.——In danger, though——terrible danger ! Italian Opera——loco focoism——gambling in stocks——Animal Magnetism——French legs——Irish heads——Maine mill sites—— Oregon building lots——phrenology——banks——brokers——twig that snapping turtle ! What are your politics ?"

" Mine, sir ? I am a federal democratic whig republican, of the loco foco genus, conservative species, whole hog in the abstract, and always ready to sacrifice personal opinion to the judicious principles of public policy, rightly understood in reference to the individual interests of the citizen. Those are my sentiments, my friend. Permit me to inquire the state of parties in Hell. Do the Whigs or Democrats rule the roast ?

—Excuse the joke ; but that puts me in mind to inquire about the firemen. How does that department vote ?"

" O, we have no people to put out fire here. We don't admit them.——They're so uncertain. But we've had our own time of it, nevertheless.——Pluto has had his hands full. Listen ! First, up gets a company of speculating ghosts, with not an obolus among the whole lot of them, and whose turn to cross hadn't come yet, and presents a petition to the throne, for an act of incorporation under the title of " The Salamander Styx Bridge, and Acheron Death and Trust Company," with banking privileges. As this was got up merely to raise the price of building lots near Colonel Tantalus' pond, which they had bought of Colonel Ixion at a high price with their promissory notes, all the loafer ghosts that had sixpence cash in their pockets, consulted and kicked. Free Trade and Sinners' Rights Associations were formed in every part of Tartarus. A special committee was sent up stairs for Fanny Wright. They contrived to get off unobserved, and the first thing we knew, down came the man giantess. The way she walked over the sulphur was a caution. She throttled Cerberus, and almost choked him with a copy of the " Emancipator," and strode on to the ferry. Seeing me half way across, she dashed into the river and came after me like a shark——upset the boat ——tumbled me and six old women and a young Baptist minister overboard, mounted the skiff, and sculled herself ashore. Soon as she landed, she stole away my boat hook, stuck upon its top her handkerchief, upon which was stamped, in indelible red ink, the motto " Equal Rights and Free Ferries——now and forever, one and inseparable." The ghosts turned pale, Acheron boiled, Tartarus trembled. Pluto came out, and took off his hat, mistaking her for Minerva on a spree. Yielding to the divine *afflatus* which possessed her he followed her into a convenient *spelunca*, and gave her audience. Here she raised the watchword cry of "Reform," and demanded that he should abandon his Pagan notion of devotion to a single wife, and that she should be made queen of Hell, No. 2. Aschalaphus standing by, ran off, on hearing the negotiation, and told Proserpine. Then there was the Devil to pay. Proserpine started, in a rage, and brought out the Fates and Furies, and rushed to the rescue of monogamy. Did you ever see women fight?—Snakes! such a row! The people in Elysium heard it, and came rushing in. Socrates and Adam Smith, Plato and Malthus flew to the rescue, with cries of "turn her out! turn her out!" "Order! Order!" sung out Pluto; but no more order could be had than on the last night of a session of Congress when Wise is speaking. Puff—puff—it's hot!"

"Well; how did you finally succeed in getting her out?"

"I can't say, my dear boy. Her ascent was as mysterious as her advent. Both immense. Some think she's here yet."

I am interrupted, my dear Editor. If you don't hear from below before, I will tell you the rest of the adventure, next time I write. Please consider this letter private.

Yours truly,   J. C., Jr.

RANDOM REMINISCENCES.

RANDOM REMINISCENCES.

EARLY TWIG-ERY.

NO. I.

DEDICATED, WITHOUT PERMISSION, TO SYLVANUS MILLER, ESQ.

> " Just as the twig is bent the tree's inclined,
>   Youth straightest stands with whip well plied behind."—POPE.

NORSWOLDWOOF, the celebrated Kamschatkan scholiast, in his " Philosophical Laconisms," which made so much noise at the time of their first publication, registered, at least, one good remark, which was rendered in Blackwood's Magazine, in strict pursuance of the original idiom—" *Times is'nt as they used to was.*" Christopher North fully appreciated the originality and beauty of the sentiment, and bestowed half a column of commendation upon its axiomatic composition. Feeling a deep impression upon my own heart of the mingled truth and pathos of the thought, I was impelled with strong desire to study what Christopher called the untranslatable original. The only copy, however, to be found in the country was in possession of the New York Historical Society,—and as to getting any book off the shelves of that institution, by a person who is not President or Secretary, or one of the Trustees ; you might as well try to get your note discounted at a bank without being one of the directors ; or perch yourself upon a high hill, with a long rake, and oyster for stars in the milky way. I tried to get elected a

4*

member, and two of my sweet cousins gave me each two shillings towards my initiation fee ; but I found that there were no meetings, and that the books were stored away for the benefit of future ages, or else laid with well-studied carelessness upon the book-tables of the literary—qu. ? *litterery* brokers—qu. ? *breakers*—men profound in books—*muslin*, and well printed—*calico ;* and who ought, therefore, to be able to appreciate such writers as Norswoldwoof—who had paid their entrance money of one hundred or five hundred dollars to buy the glory of being published in a book as gentle-men! who had got beyond b-a—k-e-r in their spelling books, and were patrons ! of the fine arts ! Heaven forgive me if I wrong them ! The heaviest affliction that I wish them is, that they will, in some moment of unnatural wisdom, pile up their hoarded cases in the park, and make a bonfire ; and re-supply their shelves with Parley's Magazine, Murray's Grammar, and Bennet's Book-keeping. Two parties will be gainers by that operation. The thirsty student, tantalized with hot thirst for the sealed-up fountains of sparkling knowledge which he grasps at in vain, may look on and see the ethereal essence of soul ascend in a curling flame, like the prophet of old, to the Heaven from which it came ; and when the burning thoughts have left the mortal scroll upon which they were impressed, he may gather and in-urn their ashes, and stellate them among his household-gods. The other party referred to will derive an advantage better appreciated by them, because more substantial. They will learn " reading, writing and arithmetic." Does any one doubt that these extensive acquirements are matters of use and adornment, of which a trader in opium, calomel, and raw-hides ought to be proud ?—Look back twenty years and tell us how many men signed their own names. Go into the register's and surrogate's offices and look at the deeds and wills executed by the ancestors of the rich. Why, a Dutchman who could WRITE was looked upon as an astrologer or necromancer ; and a stray Yankee school-master snooping out a village where he might teach young ideas how to shoot in the day-time, and the rich farmers' buxom daughters how to spell " crucifix" at night, besides keeping singing-school Saturday evening, and leading the choir in " Mear," " Wells," and " Old Hundred," on the next day, was convicted by all such young gentlemen as Abraham Bones [whose life and experience are so happily illustrated by Diedrich Knickerbocker] as no better than a juggler or an obtainer of other people's chattels under false pretences. There is a manuscript history of New York which gives an account of a justice of the peace, before whom all the causes in Duchess county were tried, who knew no touch of quill-graphy, but held his court in the woods, where the soil was loamy ; and, by the aid of his cane and certain sticks which he would set up, made his notes of the testimony, and invari-ably came to a correct conclusion.

But, alas ! " *times isn't as they used to was ;*" there is too much learning abroad. People know too much. They have studied hard names and are conceited. They carry out the advice given by our belles-lettres professor in college, and commit to memory *the names* of books they never read, and cannot be made to understand. Everybody can read. Even your Irish cook, unless she has just left her cabin in Limerick, can spell out her missal. They have got beyond " ac"—"*ac*" —" tion"—" *shion*"—" *town-shun*," and are travelling into the " *ologies*." the country is in danger of being ruined by too much " light and knowledge." These two last mentioned ambiguous names have been cracked up by all the tract and moral reform societies as being highly preferable to bread and butter ; but what have they done ? Have they demolished sin ? Have they multiplied virtue ? Are public exhibitions upon the stage of reality in Broadway, or of imitation at the Olympic, less gross and pernicious than of old ? Are the morals of the city purified ? Are we less or more like Sodom and Gomorrah than we were when I was a boy ? Men that are thirty years of age, think. Think, I say, and curse the men that taught Vice, that they might cure it, and be accounted saints ;—who first breathed into the virgin innocence of the ears of their happily ignorant wives and girls that there was such a thing as " guilt ;"—who like the serpent seducing Eve, gave Sin a name and called it " Knowledge," promising infinite happiness, while the price of the information was everlasting Hell-fire ! How smooth-tongued Belial must gloat over the idiots !

No,—" times isn't as they used to was." That's a beauty of a sentence. It has a present past, and a past present mingling in labyrinthic harmony, that fill me with rapturous pluperfection. I mount, I fly.

I am a pretty good democrat, and love the largest liberty ; but I am inclined to think that I am a little antidemonexagotheatic. I think Yankee schoolmasters ought to be taken up as vagrants. Cyphering I would permit ; but I would let no one go beyond the " rule of three." The use of hard words shall be prohibited by statute. Dictionaries are so common that boys buy them at book-auctions, and study the definitions as they carry home your marketing, and the next day you find them editors of a penny paper upon the strength of their knowing the meaning of " liberty, equality, and tergiversation." The silliest attempt at an aphorism is " *the Schoolmaster abroad*." How easy to answer it. An old settler would say, " *he'd better stay at home.*"—*Brom watch him as he goes by the orchard —are them onions all tuk up ?*"

" *Renovare dolorem,*" as my friend Ritchie says, in French, " Times isn't as they used to was." We squatted, settled, builded meeting-houses, murdered the " Six Nations,"—multiplied by twelve,—without knowing arithmetic, killed the Quakers, burned the witches, drained the meadows, cut down the trees, excommunicated the swearers, baptized the infants, courted Saturday night, kissed our wives every day but Sabbath consecrating ourlips to singing what the minister read to us upon that festival—two lines at a time,—had no hymn books —cushions neither—drew wood for the minister, tightened the cords of his bedstead, sent our boys and girls six miles to the school-house with apple-pie and plain cake according, and a rose for the school master ; ploughed, trapped skunks and buried them till they got sweet ; pigeons ! lord, fifty at a shot were nothing—rabbits, don't mention how they criticised the cabbages ; partridges ! we used to burn premature sulpher under the apple trees to save the buds ! THEN we had no schools for astronomy, chemistry and French. Every boy knew the pointers and the North Star, and he felt, moreover, when he planted his quiet little cottage, fronting the South, with his milk and cheese dairy deep in the hill side, five yards from the kitchen, that his own best-loved Katrina would have things handy.—Were not these people virtuous, good, and happy ? Yet they could not write—they could not read. Some of them, however, occasionally could spell. But of what use was reading and writing to them. Their Domine and the Squire could write their testaments and guide their timorous faith. The old Doctor could sew up their scythe-cuts and set their dislocated bones ; and the news of stirring incidents were purely, truly brought by neighbor to confiding friend. Would a christian, or an honest man, pour " the Herald," or " Exhibitions of New York as it is," into the bosoms of those ignorant lilies of innocence ? Would the God of Heaven permit Satan to spit venom upon his own radiation of beauty ?

" Times isn't as they used to was."————By-the-by,—I have been beating over ground that I did not intend to travel on—boggy—muddy,—but my dog is wild, and sometimes makes false points and wont come in. The illustration of Norswoldwoof's sentiment I intended to confine to scholastics, or the accomplishment of scholars. I can not do better than to give a touch of my own experience.

Before I begin, I want to ask a favor. I will give eighteen pence—specie—to any individual who will deliver, for me, to the Editor of the " *Spirit of the Times*," a copy of " *Webster's Spelling-book*." Don't send me the kakosyllabic monstrosity which he calls a dictionary ; I mean the old thing which he wrote before he forgot what he learned at school, and invented a new alphabet. I want the old book with the story about the green milkmaid, and of the landlord of the apple-tree stoning a boy, and the Justice deciding that Dr. Johnson's dictionary was an ox, and Noah's a Cape Cod bull —cash down.

If a gentleman of leisure were to make up his mind— that is a ridiculous expression, and I stop. Your chambermaid may " make up" your bed, after you had been beseeching multiplied pillows to give you one hour's quiet respite from a headache. Penny-liars may " make up" at a moments' warning a drowned man, a burglary, or a Corlear's-hookerism ; but *mind* has nothing to do with *manufacture*. Mind thinks, radiates. It is impulsic. It rides with the lightning *before* the wind. It flashes, and you feel the vivid flagration in your heart before you start from the burst air upon the drum of your trembling ear.

Of all the modern inventions that have brought sin and death into the world, next to Madame Lecompte's legs and Colman's engravings, the holy church doth especially anathematize Sunday Schools. They teach snotty-nosed little scarecrows what A is, truly ; and the sweet infants reward the pious zeal of their pedagogues in lisping complimentary anthems, and in committing to memory the interesting detail of the processes by which the venerable Jacob made money, and the still more pure history of the loves of David and Solomon. That is the doctrine of the Pope. You may call it his " bull," but it is not Irish only. I am Roman on this subject, and agree with the fathers that the book ought to be sealed, or else only wisely interpreted by a consecrated priest. None but a Levite should approach the altar, much less intrude into the Penetralia. Yet how is the fact in this boasted land of equal rights and equal wisdom ? Why every bastard blasphemer who can read a sentence, lays hold of the horns of the sanctuary, and butchers with impious knife his bloody victim. Walter Scott was of my opinion, when he said out of the mouth of one of his friends, " I tell thee, Elspeth, the word killeth." The literal unexplained text, whose metaphors and allegories no old women in the land can circumvent may reduce to misery the wretched soul whom it was written to beckon to salvation. The heart of diamond may be within its rough exterior, but give it unpolished, untranslated by the wise, and it will be a millstone about the neck of the outside speculator. Pope had this rivulet of thought running through his head when he wrote,

" A little learning is a dangerous thing,
  Drink deep or taste not the Pierian spring."

Are we any happier for being able to read and write ? Are we stronger, healthier, handsomer, taller, honester, than our grandsires ? Can we beard wolves in their den, and ride down perpendicularities better than old General Put ? Can we fight better than the boys did at Bunker Hill ? Can we pray more zealously and successfully than people did when every pulpit, weekly, uplifted its voice to Heaven, and obsecrated the sore smiting of the Hessians ? Will any person write a Declaration of Independence, and dare Tom Jefferson's ghost to bet and "leave it to men" which is the best. Is there any militia colonel who will accept a pair of silver pitchers for his laborious struggles through the mud of Broadway, and try to rival General Washington's address ? Yet these were the times when a man who could read and write was a great scholar. The locusts of the printing press had not yet blighted the land. The dragon's teeth of type had not been sown. If an old newspaper got, by accident, into a peaceful village, the fact was known forthwith, and the Squire engaged to investigate and read it. The sheet was looked upon suspiciously, and more thoughts dwelt upon the devil than upon the printer. The " Arabian Nights" would have had equal credence. That was not the way the Revolutionists got their news. Few could read, but all could distrust an Editor's solemn leader, because " it was in the paper." Who believed in Chatham ? Who trusted Duane ? No ! when there was a robbery, or a riot, a strike for liberty, or a row, Fame carried the report in her mouth, holding hard on a running horse. The lads rode and ran. Ah ! well ! the race of Dutch horses is extinct. " Times isn't as they used to was."

'This random prologue, written " *ad mulcendos animos*" of of the jewelry of knowledge stampers, from the apex of the regents of the university down to the base of the distributors of the Common School fund, now restores my boiler to the proper thinness of pressure. I have let off steam enough, and go ahead.

The first school I went to was a Madam's. I forget her name. She kept her brainpan in John street, opposite Dutch place. All I remember of my own acquirements is—first, the experience of a dark coal hole, under the stairway—secondly, biting pins crooked and putting them, point up, where the girls sat and wiggled,—not attending to their lessons,— and thirdly and lastly, going up before the whole school and asking the old lady, while I held tight on my posterior tegument, "*Ma'am please to let me go out?*"

Next, aunt Platt tried to teach me the humanities. A good soul was she, sixty odd, fat, pious, kind, benevolent, a lover and excuser of child-faultery. Mother she never was, but to the romping rascalities that other people sent her to adopt. And she did adopt them. She looked upon a school of thirty, and called them " MY CHILDREN." Happy labor was thine, dear aunt, for the very kindness of thy gentle punishment of looking into our eyes and speaking one word —our christian name—with those lips threatening to open, but at the same time promising not to burst apart—that little lock of oh! too soon! grey hair swelling out beneath the cap that we put in a penny a-piece to buy for thee—the gentle pressure of thy left hand, while the dexter lifted, in threat only, the smooth-shaven ferrule. No man can doubt that woman died happy. It is a solemn fact that her first bridal was her burial. She was too good for men, and slept in Heaven. She died in Dr. Spring's session room, singing,

> " Jesus lover of my soul,
> Let me to thy bosom fly."

" Hotham" was the tune.

Vol. II.—5

By this time I had acquired the alphabet, and could read.
Women's schools then began to get into bad repute, unless
they had gentlemen professors. Taste grew collegiate.
Grescom lectured on chemistry, and taught children how to
make soft soap. Tammany Hall was whitewashed, and
several sachems sent their girls to French boarding institutes.
Then commenced reform. The phrase "he can't write his
name" came into acceptation. Albums and book-tables glittered in the parlors of good society. People who couldn't
address a letter to their wives without excruciating valuable
words, affixed their certificates to reports of the West Point
examinations, vouching for the accuracy of the details, and
the supreme perfection of the students. Gammon governed
and flourished. Blessed discrimination and honesty of the
appointing power! how the retired gin-distiller, and the one
thousand per cent mixers of rhubarb and magnesia swelled
and looked wise!

In treating of Twiggery, I ought, perhaps, to order all and
classify the genera and species. I would do so, but for my
certain conviction, that no man will read this excursion who
has not, in some "pliant hour," been "licked." Every body
knows what a twig is. It is built of hickory—willow,
—that's poor, and breaks easy,—cowhide, dressed leather,
twisted eel-skin, or plaited horse-hair;—enough—enough—
my back bites the tender stripes of yet unfilled-up reminiscences. After aunt Platt was taken away, I first began to
know the modifications of twiggery. When the old woman
went to Heaven, I was sent to Picket. It was considered
necessary that my growing intellect should have some of *his*
manure upon me, and that *he* should plough and harrow my
temper. He kept his menagerie—true name, for the boys
were treated like wild beasts—in Chamber-street, near Hud-

son. He had a couple of sons for understrappers, but they were "*Dii minores.*" The old man was Jupiter, and allowed nobody else to thunder. Grim, coarse, whiskered, belly-protruding, slow of foot, quick of eye, he strode between the benches of trembling defaulters, who knew not what to call their offence, the Arbaces of heartless pedagogues. He never laughed but once. That was when he called the whole school around his throne, and announced that he had just come from the Marine Court, and had nonsuited the father of one of the little boys down stairs, in room No. 1, in an action brought against him for pummelling the infant to death. [The plaintiff's pleader made a mistake, and put in "death" in his declaration instead of "almost to death."] Then the master laughed; and when he got through, he ordered three cheers for discipline, which the boys, as they had nothing else to be cheerful about, gave clear and strong. Then the master grinned. I see his sardonic smile in my mind's eye now.

What I learned at this institute is more than I can tell. My memory goes to the cutting northeasters that rushed upon me as I turned the corner of Chamber street, and to the systematic ingenuity of the strange inventions of Picket's cruelty —"*ecce signum!*" "John Amos! come up here. I saw you, sir. Lie down." And the victim would lie upon the dirty floor at extended length, like a self-immolator before the wheels of Juggernaut. "*Shorts,* down." That made two sides of a square; to make it equilateral and complete, he would pick out boys of similar size, so that if Amos and Shorts were called down, every boy knew that Jim Cobble and Earnest Fustian were to go next. When the substratum was laid, the old man began to pile; and the human hecatombs that we sometimes made ought to be illustrated for the

benefit of all the travellers who intended to favor the world
with further dissertations upon the pyramids of Egypt.

Another quaint branch of twiggery for which this old gentleman was peculiar was his military distribution of discipline.
When he became tired of seeing and smelling the prostrate
group of culprits, squeezing the very wind out of each other
at his feet, he would order up a cohort of fresh boys, and tell
them to recite the lesson which they began to study five minutes before.   Of course they didn't know it.   A licensed
butcher would have said in one of those moments " What a
lovely sight !" and as he looked upon a dozen hands stretched
out in a long row, after the order " right dress"—" present
arms," ready to receive the broad slap of the heavy ball-bat,
taken from some " base" player, who ought to have known
too much to carry it to school !   How the old man's countenance would light up and burn with almost Mosaic fire as he
reviewed the line, firing his own *feu de joies* slap ! slam !
spank !

But I cannot help thinking that the most ingenious twiggery for which the old man is to be praised, he inflicted upon
me miserable.   It was a refinement that has made him an
honorary member of the Holy Inquisition in Rome already,
and will certainly ordain him as the cunningest cardinal in
Avernus evermore.   What the offence was for my life I cannot tell—I sincerely believe there was none, and if I did admit guilt, it was only because the tyrant frightened me.   No
matter now.   Only mark his twiggery.   I was ordered down
stairs—the school was dismissed, not a lad remained but poor
I.   " John" was despatched for " that door."   It was brought,
a veritable antique of continental times, blown off its hinges.
It was laid over the tops of the settees and desks.   I was invited to mount it, and lie upon my back in the figure of a

Saint Andrew's cross. " *Lie you there, you puppy*," said the old man. " Don't stir. *John the ropes and some coarse salt.*' They left me. Two—they seemed two hundred—long hours did I wait for my torturers. They went in to tea, and forgot me. Night closed around the empty benches, and some floor-scourer came with a lamp, and starting as at a thief, inquired " *what I was doing there ?*" I fled—fear winged my feet—desperation gave me courage. I pleaded and remonstrated with my father. I was picketed never more.

Next I went to Morse's, in Nassau street. My blessings rest upon that amiable, affectionate man. He was too mild for a *schoolmaster*, as that name is commonly " interpreted." Father—friend—brother—would be better. He accomplished by kindness what Picket could not get out by twiggery. He made us love him, for he was kind, he made us look up to him, for he was good, he made us obey him, for he was just. I never saw him in a passion. He treated children as reason-able beings, and I think he would rather have knelt at the feet of a wayward miscreant, and pleaded to him to be dutiful, than box his ears, or compass his trowsers,—which process, I re-gret to admit, with some misbegotten brats is sometimes in-dispensible.—I learned a good deal here for a boy. The greatest discovery I made was in animal physics. I learned that I had a heart—I fell in love—I never told her—with Eliza—something—not to be mentioned—who was always head of her class, and got the highest rewards of worthy com-mendation. I have seen her several times since the old school was broken up and it always put me in mind of Adam's gram-mar, and " *amo, amare, amari, amatum.*" Schoolboy dreams ; —spring lightning—meteors.

I don't precisely recollect what calamity dissolved my last referred-to apprenticeship, and consigned me to other twig-

5*

gery ; but I found myself one summer afternoon at Baskenridge, in New Jersey, boarding with old squire Lewis, in company with six or eight exurbened candidates for literary glory,
under the care of the excellent and reverend Doctor Finlay
and his man Friday—man-every-day, I ought to say—Leek.
The Doctor was a good-natured creature, and his sternness
was affected—he was a hypocrite only in pretending to be
cross. Monday mornings he regularly marched into school
with a bunch of hickory twigs, that would have adorned the
the most provident lictor in Italia. Hum ceased as the pace
began—solemn quiet looked between stealthy eyelashes. Of
whom Mr. Leek complained nobody knew. The last night's
report was quite as uncertain as the name of the next cashier
who is to be found out. Yet somebody had to be twigged, and
that we all knew. Whether it would be owing to the spiteful
malice of Leek, or to the Doctor's firm adherence to the maxim
of "spare the whip and spoil the child," we all knew that
"whack" had to come. The old man was moderate, though,
and soon lost his strength, and broke his whips intentionally,
and then went home and wrote his sermon for next Sunday,
leaving us in the care of Leek. That Leek !—Medusa is
painted with grinning snakes snapping at you from her forehead. What a husband she would have had in that usher,
with his cat-o'-sixty-nine-tails swinging from his long, lean,
foul-nailed fingers ! The personification of famine, consumption, bitterness, and spite, conglomerated and condensed !
To pull a boy's ear who was startled from his book by a flock
of pigeons skirring near the window—to catch some unfortunate in the act of laughing at an adventurous mouse intruding
into the repository of Baskenridge learning—to get a sly crack
at any boy's bottom !—that put Leek into heaven. I don't
know what salary he got, but his personal appearance was as

mean as his inside was vulgar. He perhaps had socks and a false shirt-bosom, but he stank of that horrid disease of *want of waterism*. He was a decided loafer. He mistook his vocation, and should have established himself in the calamus pond near the school-house, and watered with the bloodsuckers. He might have thus avoided the prospective reputation which Ovid wrote for him, referring to his pulling juvenile hair, and scraping for rare love in monkeys' heads, and finding none but of the entomological species—

"Unguibus et raras vellentem dentibus herbes."

I gathered here, however, more than I learned in any eighteen months before. Principal, was wickedness, and secondary, smooth-faced falsehood. The one followed the other, as Lucifer's tail courses—no, streams—sticks—arrow-pointed hisses after its master's hands—" heads !"—" after" —not so. I found that I was a simple goose when my father left me, and drove back, leaving me his paternal blessing, with a shilling to buy fish-hooks, and that I " didn't know nothing." I was no scholar, and the whole lot of boys was on me with tricks, practices, and levies innumerable and scandalous. I stood it until my eyes got opened, and then I fought. It was a Philadelphia boy ; let him deny it. I did do it—and the whole school saw it—Jim Black stood by.—Poor Jim's dead. But it was effectual—my reputation was established, and nobody dared to follow my tracks, and let down my figure—y —4's in the great swamp, or the parsonage woods, or touch my reed-pole floating for catfish in Doty's pond. Leek was the only enemy that could smite me. His inflictions I took as a matter of duty, or perhaps habit, just as I now take sugar to my coffee, and salt to my beefsteak. The frolics and the mimic deviltry of that school after I got into " the cabinet," I have not time to record now. Wisdom crowned my forehead, and know-a-thing-or-two-or-osity sparkled in the centre of the diadem.

With such acquisitions, I was brought home and sent to blind Joe Nelson to prepare for college. I looked at Joe, and Joe felt me. He had *his* instrument of twiggery in his hand at the time, consisting of a thong of leather, between which and his hand there was an electrical sympathy; and with that he seemed to feel the condition of my flesh, and estimate what possible twiggery it could bear. His blue, bright, lightless eyes knew nothing; but his whip saw. Certain it is, its accurate stripes made delinquents wish they had a lightning-rod to carry the fiery streak down from their non-conducting shoulders, and precipitate into the earth their hot sufferance of random vengeance. John Walsh, the junior partner, or head clerk, looked on with both his foreheads, and all his chins, and grinned his satisfaction. Then we all studied out aloud. "Double, double, toil and trouble," snakes, witchcraft, Greek, and algebra were all studied at together. The essence of the sound, if condensed by a curious chemist, would have been a mixture to be named. We were examined and admitted as freshmen in Columbia. I laid my cheek upon the bosom of Alma.

I must rest now, I am upon holy ground. Discuss we this new culture of twiggery with solemn awfulness. I am exalted to the upper air. Base cuffs, vanish!

EARLY TWIG-ERY.

NO. II.

REMINISCENCES OF OUR CLASS IN COLLEGE.

" Whoever has to College been,
Must surely know the joy, Sir,
To see old Granny prose and grin,
And flatter every boy, Sir.
Yankee Doodle, you have spoke
With great propriety, Sir,
You are a credit to yourself,
And honor unto me, Sir."

THAT is a torn chaplet from the festive wreath, which thou, dear Doctor Bill T——, didst fling upon the altar of our affections, on that roysterous night, when we solemnized a wake over the corpse of the class of eighteen hundred and—blank. The smoke of the incense of the altar went up gloriously.

It was a melancholy, frolicksome, mad symposium. Commencement was ended. The speeches had been spoken. The berries and the leaves of the bacca-laureation had been plucked. Each ingenuous youth had got his due share of " *tu vero videas, probe te geras*,"* to start him ahead upon his journey through this world of trouble. The attentive audience had been dismissed with thanks for their civil behavior,

---

* Part of the President's charge when he enacts the solemnity of making an A. B., and gives the diploma on commencement day,—copied from the dedicatory injunction used by Pope Benedict XIV., on the installation of Black Nuns.

and a benediction in Latin. We were let loose to *seek* our fortunes. The blessing of our Alma Mater was fresh upon our heads, the memory of the happy days we had labored in her household was green and bitter in our hearts. We had her best recommendation for sobriety, honesty, and extensive capacity, in our pockets. "*Optimæ spei juvenis,*"* was wreathed around our brows. We were proud, and humbled, happy and wretched. The new sense of boyhood gone, and manhood begun, of not understood independence, crazed us. We walked on stilts.——We felt the earth pressing down upon us as on a clod.——We were newly married.——We had lost our mother.——The tie was severed.——We were turned out of house and home.——We should never be called before the board again.——We had been torn from the breasts of our beautiful nurse, and from the blessed fountains whence we had been accustomed to suck our daily milk of Greek particles, and conic sections, and were thrown into the streets to make room for a new set of brats whom the professors had been lately getting! We were collegians no more! Good bye, black silk gown. Good bye, old trees. Good bye, bell. Good bye, janitor. But not yet had we said, Good bye, fellows. A very afflicting valediction had been pronounced for us, in the church, it is true, and much tears were talked of, by a speaker appointed by the board. But that appointment was not ours, and the pathos reached the hearts of other classes than the senior. *Our* valedictory orators pronounced, and sung, their *valete*, at Kensington House, where our parting supper was spread. We were all orators, and poets too, that night. But chiefly thee, Dear Doc, did Anacreon fill full of inspiration. Why wert thou at the foot of thy class, O thou Son of Song!

* The common complimentary lie in the diploma.

The declared estimate of merit of boy students does not always stellate either the honesty, or discrimination of the judges. I do not say this out of bad spite because I carried away none of the honors. My vexation is that such excellent merit as the Doctor's should have borne off what is next to disgrace. But no matter, dear Bill; thou wert up head in our love; and it is better to have warm, full hearts, without honors, than a cold, empty honor without a share in your classmates affections. Remember, too, that gigantic Dr. Mitchell was accounted worthy to be graduated in an equal rank. And thou wert comforted with the companionship of Junius T——, and Jack T——, forming with thee, a goodly musical T. party; all since, solemn medical doctors. Jun. and Jack, alas! breathe no more the atmosphere of this earth. They are with the school-fellows of Justice Silence. Years since, ye died, boys, in your yet unexhausted adolescence. *Pax vobiscum!* How many of us are left? Let us call the roll, and see.

Shall we call the roll of the dead, and demand our friends from the grave? Aye! let us bring back the old college chapel, and the familiar lecture-rooms, and the healthy youth that defied mortality with its well-knit muscles, and the sport and the loves of boy enthusiasm. Classmates, come! Attention to the calling of the roll! ADSUM is the word.

HARRY P.!——HARRY P.!—Thou wert at the head of thy class worthily. But thou answerest not now to thy name called. Thy place is empty, and we must mark thee " absent." O sorrow! not for thee, but for us who mourn so much genius and virtue lost to us!

Noble, magnanimous, proud Harry! A boy patriot, stately, exclusive, jealous of his right of citizenship, heir of a rich estate, distrustful of the common herd, hater of Irishmen!

He worshipped Hamilton. But the grave holds him now, whom the Senate-house expected ;——his body only, not his fame. Death, not Oblivion, has triumphed. Before the Destroyer came he honored his country, and kissed the soil of Greece dear to him for his love of her heroes and philosophers. He comforted blood-stained Marathon, and, danger-daring, dealt out the charities of his country to the suffering islands of the Ægean. The Turk cursed him, and the bread which he brought to the lips of the daughters of Pindar and Demosthenes.

Harry wrote his travels and experience. But he was modest, and he did not write for lucre, eking out his landlord's rent by "inklings" spattered from a bitten pen. No printer's devils, bought with unknown clean shirt-collars, extolled the praise of his unaffected story. His book knew no puffs, and has been only a thing to steal from. But he is honored where his spirit would have sought honor, and it matters not that the million of ladies'——weekly——miscellanies never had communion with his spirit.

BILL J.——No. 2, answers " here," and we give hearty thanks for the hope that some good fellows are left to us. Three years and a half did studious, always prepared Billy, wear the crowning laurels of laborious desert ; but he laughed, one day, out of season, during the senior year, and " *alter*,"——Harry,—— " *tulit honores*." He was saved the necessity of writing a salutatory in Latin——he abjured the past, and the present, and consoled himself with a poem on " the pleasures of anticipation." It is a thing to be recorded and rejoiced at, that his anticipations were bright, and better yet, that they have not been fashions of deceitful fancy. The purest ermine on his neck, gives ample vouchers for his acknowledged excellence.

Bill is the same Bill yet ;——simple, but wise ;——unpretending, but learned ;—single-hearted,—guile never knew him, nor uneasy envy. To do what would make him happy,—that was his only exertion ; and he never was happy, but in doing good, or in helping along some piece of doubtful evil which was needful for the comfort of his friends. You cannot provoke him, nor make him jealous. He looked sorrowful for only two minutes, when he heard the annunciation of his lost first honor. It would not grieve him now, to be defeated by one vote, in a contest for a seat in Congress. Put Woodfall and the Revised Statutes under his arm, and he is the same boy that he was when he went down Park Place, hugging Euclid, Vince, and Greca Majora.

Next—next—next ;——I never did exactly comprehend the adjustment of the honors of scholarship in our class ;—but next, I believe, comes the Vale—dictator—I stand by that word. It means a dictator appointed by the board of professors, to take care that the boys bid each other good-bye before the ladies and gentlemen, according to the forms of the bye-laws of the college, for that purpose duly established and enacted.

I have forgiven thee, O careful minder of rules and regulations, obedient, good boy ; and I love thee, now, moderately. Yet it was a pity, that, of all the class, thou only wert present on that morning when I was doomed to read, in the chapel, after prayers, before the assembled college, with crocodile penitence, a sorrowful admission of the enormity of my adjudged iniquity, and to exalt the merciful mildness of the retribution ! Thy presence spoiled the *oneness* of the effect. The freshmen, too, might have mistaken thee for the culprit, or coupled thee with me, miserable as a joint transgressor. But the offence was not very rank, and they could not have held thee disgraced. I protest that that punishment was cruel

VOL. II.—6

and unusual.   So thought my classmates ; and I being ignorant, and utterly innocent of conspiracy, they resolved to be
absent on the morning of the execution.*

* It is no more than justice to myself to state what was the offence.   I
therefore give an original record, being the half-burned rough minutes of the
trial, picked up by me in the college yard, and which the janitor had, probably, incautiously swept out of the President's room.   I give also a copy
of the letter which the good old man sent to my father, for the purpose of
making sure of my attendance at the time and place to which the ceremony
was postponed.   The letters are perfect models in their way—safe prece-
dents.   The record is half consumed, but I give a *fac-simile* of its remains.

irreverent be-
" Cypress appeared before the board on a charge of disturbing *   *
the
of the Chapel by talking ; which fact being fully proved ig- *   *   *
also
of several of several the professors & partially admitted *   *   *   *   *

board after mature deliberation sentenced him to di—   *   *   *   *   *
and not to be received by him
-tion until he had made such acknowledgment   *   *   *   *   *   *   *

and ats as the board should consider satisfactory."
The following is the President's epistle, scilicet.

King's Coll., Shrove Tuesday.
" SIR—Your son, J. Cypress, Jr , signed an acknowledgement of his incorrect behavior during the religious exercises of the Chapel, which he was
to have read on Tuesday last ; but perceiving that most of his classmates
were then absent, I deferred his reading it until I should have an opportunity of informing the class of the consequence of a combination to resist the
authority of the College.   I have given them that information, and have
ordered their attendance in the Chapel at prayers to-morrow, when I shall
expect your son to appear and read the reasonable acknowledgment he has
subscribed.   I have thought it my duty to make this communication to you,
being assured that your son cannot fail to profit by your good advice on this
occasion.   " With great respect, Your ob't serv't.

" To J. Cypress, Senior, Esq."
Now follows the writ of " intrabit in executionis locum" which put me
in the pillory ; to wit :—
" REV'D SIR,—It is with pain that I learn that my son has been guilty
of incorrect behavior during the religious exercises of the chapel.   Be assured that it meets my decided disapprobation.   A sense of our unworthi-
ness when we approach the presence of the Sovereign of Heaven and
Earth in prayer ought to affect our hearts with due solemnity.   I regret

God bless their noble souls! Only thou wert there, sitting with meekness and sweet humility, and pitying, doubtless, those bad young men who imposed it upon thee to represent the virtue of the class, and to reap the meed of the contrast of thy good behavior;—like Hogarth's good apprentice, who married his master's daughter, and got the estates and honors of the family.

Verily, good boys shall have their reward. Prosperity shall still follow *thee*, O my friend!—assiduous, watchful, vain, subtle, obsequious to the People,—the People shall yet own thee for a mighty man to get office from them.

Let us go on with the roll. P. M. is called and comes; and we clasp to our bosom the spirit of poetry and the soul of friendship. He was the favorite of the class, the prized-and admired. What sensibility of criticism, or what instability of purpose, dearest P., deprives the class of the honor of thy name, long since by heaven decreed to be celebrated for mighty genius.

By his side, coming with modest steps, approaches amiable STEPHEN H. His thin form, pale cheek, light blue eye,—his pleasantly smiling, half opened lips, disclosing small brilliantly white teeth, are familiar and welcome as heretofore. Only he is older, and there is a cast of care upon his brow, deeper,

the trouble he has given you, and the disgrace he has brought upon himself, and I pray God that the discipline imposed upon him will have a salutary effect. He has my orders to attend the chapel to-morrow morning, and comply with your directions. Indisposition has prevented his attendance to-day, which I hope you will excuse. Your ob't serv't,

J. CYPRESS.

" To ————————
" Pres. King's Coll.

That is the kind of Twiggery administered to boys when they get into College, and are called " Gentlemen." Twiggery for small boys is only milk and water. This is imperial tea.

and half melancholy.   Happy is that village church which owns him for her pastor.

Next, jolly I. F. dashes to his place, and we greet his rosy face with the well-remembered joy of old times.   He first gave his heart to the study of the decisions of Courts that have powers to overrule the established fashions of other brother and sister tribunals, and which are commonly called " Law ;" but soon, and wisely, determined that the whole race of Bracton and Britton were unprofitable company ; and now he draws a revenue from rum, sugar and molasses.   Mark him " present" with a whole heart.

BILL B. cannot speak.   Consumption wasted away him, beloved both by the professors and his fellow-pupils.   Weep not.   It is the common lot.   We have all got to go soon. Call on.

J. S. gives an uncertain sound.   His voice is as the voice of a ghost, or else as of a schoolmaster buried alive in the far west.   I know not how to mark him.

Good-hearted S. O., too.   He left his country, and pursued the lucre of merchandize in a foreign land.   Does the sunny sky, or the cold earth of the churchyard canopy his head. He is absent without excuse.

H. J., solemn and dignified for a little fellow, wears a bishop's cassock, and seems to censure the freedom with which we summon old associates ; but he takes his seat and submits to our invocation.

G. W. flourishes with the scalpel and lancet.   Impatient haste draws him to his patients.   We must let him depart. He is one of the friends to whom we might give authority in an extreme case to *cut us*, but then, only professionally.

G. H. ministers to the reformed Dutch in a pleasant town n Jersey.   When I saw him last, some years ago, he had given proof of his power of persuasion, by inducing a prime lamb of his flock to become his spouse ; and she had given fruitful evidence of her attachment to the shepherd, in the shape of half-a-dozen little lambkin boys and girls.

F. P. comes next, true gentleman, from his magnificent manor, nor avoids a seat with his classmates, who always received him open-armed. Goddess Fortune, when she smiled upon him, took off her bandage and exercised good judgment.

G. G. rather majestic at some times, but always good-natured. G. cries out a hearty " here." He worshipped the legal muses, and still officiates in their priesthood, speaking oracles to clients, who, with just confidence, pay well for favorable responses.

W. C. leaps into his place with a long bound ;—he whom we used to call " Amaryllis,"—with his soft, feminine cheek, clear gentle eye, and beginning-to-grow downy chin. He was famous for a quick moving foot, and was always chosen first at foot-ball. I have to show a scar upon my knee, gained from him upon the Battery, in the raging melee. The class got through trigonometry while I was laid up, and that consoled me. He plays now the serious games of " *for that whereas,*" and " *may it please your Honor.*" The boy ball-player has disappeared in the Counsellor of men.

The list is nearly through ; Death has made sad havoc below the middle of the class. There are left, besides, to answer only W. M. and W. G., bred to the legal bar, but happily independent upon that laborious profession ;—and then, dear *Doctor Bill*, and E. P., of unquestionable talent and laziness, Nimrod of the class,—mighty feather scatterer. We awarded to him the first honor in that department of science, which comprises the theory of percutient bodies, and the composition and resolution of forces and projectiles. That kind

6*

of philosophy was truly natural to him—he was born to illustrate it.   I never knew a practical lecturer who, "the initial
velocity being given," could better "find the direction in which
a body must be projected in order to hit a given point."   He
is high yet on some kind of "*points*," and almost inimitable as
to "direction."

Let us not forget C. E., honored with a diploma, *causa fa-
voris*, and the payment of the necessary fees ;—nor simple
G. S., "*commee*," as his name went.   He was the jovial An-
dronicus of the class, yet was sometimes pathetic, and read
compositions about "the streaming rivulet of consistency
which flows but to cement," and other poetical melancholies
of the same tender spirit.   Commee paid the fees, however,
and got his diploma.   Money is a great blessing.   Where the
boy is now the Lord knows.   Mark him absent.

What horrid appetite of the grave has swallowed up the
rest of the three last grades !   Little, hump-backed P. S., and
red-haired Tom K., and strong-passioned E. S., and thin J. L.,
torn from the church, and fat "Duck" W., and pale, innocent
shadow W. F., who answered to the *sobriquet* of "Sol Lob,"
and musical Jack T., with his ever-present companion Jun. ?
——Alas! boys—

> "You are not here ! the quaint witch Memory sees
> In vacant chairs, your absent images,
> And points where once you sat, and should be now,
> But are not.—I demand if ever we
> Shall meet as then we met ?"——SHELLEY.

Stay! stay! stay! stay!   I recall my invocation !   Speak
not, I conjure you !   Speak not !   My heart is gone !   I cannot bear the solemn vision !

*   *   *   *   *

What fearful changes are produced by the revolution of a
few short years !   We entered, a class of forty-seven.   We

were graduated, a class of twenty-nine ; of this number only nineteen are surviving, counting some bachelors as existing of whom I have no certain knowledge ! It seems but as yesterday that we were boys ; and now we are mature men, clergymen, physicians, lawyers, merchants, judges, legislators, fathers in the Republic ! It never occurred to me before that I am getting old. It is time for me to repent and reform. Dr. Wilson used to say that our class was the worst class that he ever had to do with, and he was pleased to assure me upon one occasion that I was the worst young " mon" in it. I wonder whether I have improved any. But he did me injustice there, I never threw a torpedo on the floor between the Doctor's legs, merely to see him jump, nor did I ever let loose in the lecture-room a mouse, or any other quadruped, as did some sad boys with longer faces, and in better credit than myself. I seriously affirm that my only guilt has been that of an accessory after the fact, in laughing at the silly joke. Yet I had not occasionally to suffer for *imputed* transgressions, as thou, dear Doc., canst testify. But I never quarrelled with thee, Doc., about that matter—and it is all over now. Let the thing go.

Here I am ! here I am ! And what am I, that I am left to write these reminiscences ? Where is my recorded merit, my service done to the church, or to my country, of which this prolonged duration of life is the reward ? Let me retire, and give myself an examination. I am, I think, awakened.

A FEW INTERESTING INCIDENTS IN THE TERRESTRIAL EXISTENCE OF A YOUNG MAN WHO USED TO LIKE HORSES.

I LOVE a good, fast horse. I luxuriate in a well balanced buggy. If my biograghy be ever written, "*gaudet equis*" will be the weathercock quotation set above the history to show which way the wind of its lucubration is about to blow. My equine propensities were developed as soon as I could toddle upon truant feet to the nearest stable in the neighborhood. At the sixth year's existence, I abstracted a shilling from my stepmother's work box, to pay the man that kept the zebra ; but I honestly paid it back, with funds acquired the next day by running away from school and holding the horses of two militia colonels, when they dismounted on the parade ground, for a grand review by the brigadier general.

Our milk-man had a horse ; he was not a very especial beauty ; but couldn't he go fast around the corner ! I once knocked down a little peanut girl, and turned Maiden-lane into a very palpably milky way, by trying to find the maximum of proximity which might be attained between a pump and the hub of a wheel, without any necessary collision of contiguous particles of matter. Like many other philosophers, I came near sacrificing my life to my scientific zeal, just at the moment when I deemed my discovery secure, and my triumph certain and glorious. The jealous fates, as usual, interfered, and with violent rage at my promised success, precipitated me across the street into the centre of the peanut establishment just referred to. Down went the lady-merchant, and down went her apples, peanuts and barbers'-poles. I felt sorry for the poor thing, but it was all her fault, for not getting out of the way ; or else it was the fault of the corporation in planting such a stubborn hydrodynamical obstacle at the corner of the street.

This was but the preface to more glorious exploits, the entitulement of a long chapter of. spirit-stirring accidents. The incidents of my life have been but a catalogue of the names of danger. I have been run away with by frightened, and kicked and bitten by vicious steeds ; I have been thrown from stumblers ; I have broken down in sulkies ; I have been upset in gigs—in fine,—for the whole catalogue would be tedious,—I have been crushed, and banged and bruised, and battered in all manner of imaginable fashions ; so that it is a crying mercy that I have fingers left to write this penitential confession. Indeed, when I reflect upon my various hairbreath salvations, I cannot help thinking of what an eminently amiable Dutch gentlewoman told certain foraging pupils of a country boarding-school, concerning some choice forbidden fruit, touching which we had mounted a tree in her garden. " Don't hook them are cherries, boys," she screamed, " I'me resarved them for presarves." O ! what a jubilate would go up from my blessed maiden aunts, were the promise of a hope to be shadowed forth, that I am reserved for some better function than to moisten the shears of Mistress Beldame Atropos !

When I had escaped so far as my sixteenth year, I was driving a spirited, half-broken colt before a pleasure wagon, near a country village, in the neighborhood of which myself and my companion expected to shoot on the succeeding day. It was just at night, and our journey was nearly completed. All of a sudden, our whiffle-tree became detached from the vehicle, and fell upon the horse's heels. Off then he started, in the madness of his fright, utterly uncontrollable, and whirling us after him in the bounding wagon. The trees and fences appeared and vanished like lightning; we seemed to fly. All that I could pray for, was to be able to keep our racer in the road, and I hoped to hold him on a straight and steady run, until the furious animal should be exhausted. Vain hope! my hands were soon powerless from the strain of holding and sawing and pulling on the reins. Just at this crisis, a little green lane, running at right angles with the turnpike, invited the wilful feet of our crazy colt, by a fair promise of an easy road, and a speedy barn-yard termination. But, alas! not three bounds had the runaway made upon his new chosen course, before he brought us upon a spot where they were mending the track, and where the way was accordingly strewn with huge, rough stones. That was the last I saw, and it is all I remember of the matter.

Two days afterwards, I awoke, and found myself in bed, in a strange place. I raised my hand to rub my eyes open, and dispel the supposed dream, but to my astonishment, I found that my arm was stiff and bandaged, as though I had been lately bled. I was weak and sore in all my bones. There was a smell of camphor in the room. A bottle marked " soap liniment," stood upon a table by my bed-side. The window-shutters were half closed, but a curiously cut crescent,—the crowning glory, no doubt, of the artificer of the domicil,—admitted the bright rays of a mid-day sun. All was still as the solitude of a wilderness.

I fell back upon the pillow in amazement. It was a neat, pleasant, little room, plainly, but comfortably furnished, adorned with peacocks' feathers, tastefully arranged around the walls, and a large boquet of fresh flowers in the fire-place. The appointments of the bed were delightful; the sheets were white as snow, and the curtains were of old-fashioned chintz, blue and white, presenting to my wondering eyes innumerable little venuses and cupids. Why should I be a-bed there, and the sun shining in the window, bright as noonday ?

A newspaper lay upon the foot of my bed ; I took it up, and gazed upon it vacantly. It was the village hebdomodal, just moist from the press. A mist floated before my eyes as they fell upon my own name. When I regained my uncertain vision, I made out with difficulty to comprehend the following editorial announcement : " We regret to mention, that on Thursday evening last, a serious accident befell Mr. Renovare Dolorem, jun. and Dr. Cerberus Angelo, of New-York, as they were riding in a wagon, in the vicinity of this village. The horse taking fright, ran away, upset the vehicle, and threw out the gentlemen near the toll-gate. Mr. D. was taken up for dead, but the doctor escaped unhurt. Fortunately, Squire Hoel Bones was passing by at the time, and he and the doctor conveyed Mr. D. to a house in the neighborhood, where, we are happy to say, every attention is rendered to the unfortunate sufferer. Mr. D. continues still insensible."

Here then was a development of the why and wherefore of my stiff joints and meridian repose. " So, then, now for another week's repentance," I sighed aloud ; but there was some one at the door, and I stopped and shut my eyes. I heard the rustling of frocks, and soft footsteps fell upon the floor, and presently the curtains were drawn aside, and I perceived the shadows of two light figures bending over me, and I heard low, restrained breathings. A small forefinger wandered about my wrist, in search of my pulse ; a little hand was drawn several times across my forehead, and then it put back the tangled hair that overhung my eyebrows : I thought it seemed to linger about my temples, as though its owner wished there was another matted tuft yet to be adjusted.

" He has got more color than he had, sister ;" was the first spoken sentence.   No reply was made.

" Poor fellow ! I wonder if he will die. Is n't he handsome, Mary ?" said the same fair speaker, after a little pause.

I am telling a true story, and if I have to rehearse compliments that were paid me when a boy, it must not be set down under the head of vanity.

Mary answered not, but she sighed. - That was voice and speech enough for me. She was evidently the younger of the two, and my boyish fancy quickly formed the beau ideal of the girl who heaved that sigh for my misadventures and dangers. I was at once in love, deeply, devotedly. I cared not to open my eyes ; I would willingly have been blind for ever, the vision of my imagination was so happy. Yet it was painful to lie there, a hypocrite, affecting insensibility, and hear my physiognomy and my chance of recovery discussed between the maidens. Perhaps I was bashful—*O quantum mutatus !* and had not the courage to encounter the eyes of beings whom I knew not, but in the kind discharge of the grateful offices of guardian angels. I wonder they did not feel my quick beating pulse, and hear my throbbing heart beating against my ribs !

Presently they left my bed-side and glided to the looking-glass, where they conversed in inaudible wispers. I ventured to peep through a crevice in the curtain, and reconnoitre my gentle nurses. Need I say they were both beautiful ?

Presumptuous wretch !   O ! worse than profaner of the mysteries of the Bona Dea, to gaze with unlicensed eye upon the delicate services of the toilet !   The cruelly punished Actæon was to be pitied, for he rushed unwittingly into the presence of the hunter goddess ; but I courted my just punishment, and if I was doomed to love both sisters madly, it was but a merciful judgment!

The elder sister was, I thought, about twenty; Mary had scarcely passed her fifteenth year. Had it not been for that newspaper, I might have revelled in the fancies of a Turkish paradise.

Jenneatte took out her comb, and there gushed down her back a full bright flow of auburn tresses, that almost reached her feet.

Sister Mary assisted her in plating and adjusting and putting them up, and then tightened her corset-lacing, and then ————, spare me, spare me, too faithful memory! and then sister Jenneatte left Mary and me alone.

If the doctor had come in at the moment, he could have told whether I had a fever, without taking out his watch, and looking wise.

I closed my eyes, for Mary was at my bedside, and her evident agitation assured me that there was pity in her heart. Kind, good girl! that innocent sympathy would have won the mercy of the coldest censor. She put her arm under the pillow, and gently raised my head. Something rested on my cheek; it was warm and moist; there was a gentle pressure about it; it was still and quiet; and Mary's breath was with it; and it came again, and again—yes, Mary kissed me— gods!

Fudge. I am getting rhapsodical. What can have made my eyes so misty? Mary is nothing to me—now that————, pshaw!

When Doctor Cerberus Angelo came in to see me, I was alone, tossing to and fro with a burning fever. Consternation and hurry were written on his face, for he came upon a summons from Mary, who had told him, in tears, that I had waked up, and was very wild and flighty.

The lancet renewed its office, and sudorifices and antifebriles were again my bitter portion. But all the doctor's practice reached not my disease. That night, that night! how I suffered! I raved and ranted all manner of incoherent nonsense; now calling upon Mary, and now crying for Jenneatte. The doctor soothed, and scolded, and brought me mint tea, and swore at me. At last, I fell asleep, and there was a quiet house until the next morning, when I awoke faint, weak, and melancholy.

I tried to reason with myself upon the absurdity of my passion for the two girls, but without avail. It was a species of insanity which I could not cure. I slowly recovered my strength and health, but before a fortnight had elapsed, I had offered my boy-heart to each of the sisters, and was engaged to be married to them both.

This was not villainy, but madness. The doctor found it out, and read me a lecture on gratitude. I think he was jealous of me. He wrote also to my father, and a close carriage soon conveyed me from the place where my heart was doubly pledged. Jenneatte kissed me good-by at the door. She could do it with propriety—she was so much older than me; but Mary ran up into her room, to cry, by herself.

When I arrived at man's estate, did I not of course continue to love Mary, and make the tender-hearted little country girl my wedded wife?——

I am wandering again. Let me proceed to another incident. We were talking of horses and accidents.

——

I am romantic enough to love to ride upon a moonlit night.

What a beautiful sight is the full, round-faced goddess, mounting into a clear, blue sky, just after the snow has done falling, and the wind is lulled into an almost infant's breath! How it makes one think of sleigh-bells, and fur cloaks, and buffalo skins, and mulled wine, and bright eyes, and cold elastic cheeks, and warm merry hearts! "On such a night as this," my college chum Harry and I drove a gallant pair of coursers up to old Dorus Van Stickler's mansion, in New-Jersey. The girls had promised to go, and the sleighing was capital, and there was to be a ball at Valley-grotto, about nine miles off. We left the horses in charge of sable Sam, and bounded into the house. Harry's sweetheart was all ready, but Jemima my Jemima had a bad headache, and could not go. This grief was distressing enough, in all conscience ; but what think you of her aunt Starchy's stalking into the room, rigged out with muff and tippet—as I am a sinner!—and telling me that it was a pity that I should be disappointed, and that she would go with me herself, in Mima's place ?

Fire and ice! what benevolence! and O! provident antiquity! she put into my hands as a pledge of her sincerity, her snuff-box, and a towel-full of gingerbread, to sneeze and eat upon the road.

I was patient ; very patient. Yet, nevertheless, I did think of going out and breaking one of the horses' legs. "But after all," whispered my good genius to me, and then I to Harry, "what need we care! To be sure, we can't go to the ball, and we'll have to come home early ; but trust to fate. I'll try to get rid of her. Remember, *I* shall drive."

I assisted the old lady into the sleigh. It was like lifting an icicle or a chesnut rail.

We rode more than a mile before a word was spoken, except to the horses. I had the reins. Harry and his loved

one were on the back seat, talking by looks and actions.
Happy, happy Harry !

The old woman, after a while, grew drowsy—she did, by
Jove.   She pitched backwards and forwards, now knocking
Harry, and now saluting me with her honored cranium.   She
seemed used to it, for despite of all my hopes, she would not
tumble out of the sleigh.

At last we approached a tavern, near which was a beautiful, deep snow-drift.   I knew the ground.   It was rough, and
a little precipitous on the roadside, and unless I drove with
uncommon carefulness, we should certainly be upset.   I
looked at Harry.   There was a contagious wickedness in his
eye that made my hand unsteady.   I must have pulled on the
near-side rein a little too hard, for the runner went down into
a deep rut, our centre of gravity was lost, and we were un-
ceremoniously tumbled helter-skelter into the snow-bank.

Aunt Starchy screeched out, as though every bone in her
body was broken.   Harry lifted her up, and brushed the snow
off her, while I got the horses into the road.   She insisted
upon going to the tavern, to ascertain whether she had not
received some inward bruise, declaring, in spite of all our entreaties, that she would ride no further, and that we must go
on without her.

Accordingly, we hoisted her in, and drove up to Boniface's.
The first thing that I did there, was to get her a stiff glass of
gin and water, which the old lady drank off with great comfort
to her weak stomach, declaring that she always admired
how considerate I was.   This prescription being so well received, I was satisfied that a hot rum-toddy might be swallowed with additional benefit ; and I am proud to declare that
my course of practice upon this occasion made the most rapid

and successful progress. The good old gentlewoman soon ceased to grunt, and she presently fell into a pleasant sleep.

It would have been cruel to awake her and renew our entreaties to accompany us ; so we tucked her up, and told Mrs. Boniface we would call for her when we came back, and off we started for the ball. O! had Jemima but been with us, then ! However, little Sue de Mott and Jane Antonides both lived on our road.

Every body has been on a sleighing frolic once, and it would be foreign to our business, to tell what else took place. Harry stopped for the old lady on his return about three o'clock next morning. Something detained me in the neighborhood of the ball-room until daylight.

Riding of a dark stormy night cannot be esteemed a pleasure. Yet a frequent roadster must sometimes be prepared to say composedly to the clouds, " pour on, I will endure." My last experience of a wet ride was shared by Doctor Gulielm Belgium. Fate has been ironical with me, in more than once giving me a doctor for a companion in my travelling distresses. I told this story once to Angelo, in a letter which I have begged back to help my memory. I cannot do better than to quote my recital on the impulse of the adventure. Here it is.

" ——So he invited me to take some vehicular enjoyment on the road to Cato's.

" Allons ! and we started.

" He was made up with more than even his own exquisiteness, this afternoon. His mere vestimental arrangements were enough to show that in his time he had read a book, and travelled out of his county. There was nothing flash or Corinthian in the structure ; the order of the architecture was

7*

rather of the simplest Doric.   But what a beautiful fitness!
what a harmony of composition!   He had crowned his caput
with a bran new golgotha, beneath whose gracefully curved
brim, his late shorn locks showed here and there their glossy
edges, just sufficiently to satisfy the careless gazer of the ample
stock from which they descended, and without encroaching too
much upon the boasted beauty of his well-framed forehead.
His whiskers—they were so accurately and curiously cut, you
would have been reminded of the days when people trimmed
trees and hedges into the likeness of birds and beasts ; they
were so thick, and smooth, and regular, that a stray mosquito
planting his tired feet upon their tangling meshes, might have
thought himself upon the surface of a swath of his own native
meadows, just after it had been swept by the scythe of the
merry mower.   His cheek had a ruddy, hearty glow of health
upon it.   His eye was bright and keen.   You would have
thought it had not twinkled over hochheimer for a month.
But the *coup de grace* of all was a kidded forefinger, against
which gently pressing digital there seemed to languish a slen-
der walking-stick, of the most singular and severe virtue.   No
vulgar man ever sported such a staff.   There was but one
other like it in the world.   It was the rarest quality of sandal-
wood, precious as the golden rod, that led the pious Æneas
to the elysian fields.   It cost judgment, taste and a price.   It
was of eastern origin, and drew its earliest breath in India.
You might have suspected that, from the voluptuous perfume
that was breathed from the wood, and from its delicate form
and tint, and from the fineness of its texture and fibre.   The
color was slightly changeable, and nearest of any thing else
to the invisible orange of the neck plumage of a Barbary
pheasant.

" None but a brave man, and a good-looking, well-dressed fellow would have dared to wear it.

" We reached our original destination in safety, and then, tempted by the mildness of the evening, extended our jaunt in the pleasant twilight to Harlaem, and returned at our easy leisure to the Roman's. Here a sudden and violent midnight-black mass of rain and thunder and lightning blocked up the road, so that we were fain compelled to stop and comfort ourselves with tongue and a salad. When the storm abated, we renewed our travel homeward, Belgium commanding the reins. Soon, however, again the darkness became so thick, that it rested upon our eyelids like a palpable weight ; we could not see our way except when the heavenly fulgurations set it all on fire. Still on we went. There is a place about two hundred yards from the censor's, on the return to the city, where the alderman of the twelfth ward has provided a deep ditch on the roadside, for the devil to set man-traps. I had a feint recollection of the existence of these pitfalls, and I entreated my learned friend to let me have the reins.

" B. was a good fair-weather driver, and one of the few whom I could trust by daylight ; but he had not the owl eyes of an old traveller by night. His pride, however, stood up at the insinuation that I could see better in the dark than he, and he peremptorily refused.

" Of all the agonies of apprehension, save me from the incubus of an unskilful, head-strong driver ! I begged and beseeched him to yield, for I saw that he was leaving the road ; but no, he insisted that he was right, and that he could not be mistaken.

" ' Drive to the right, for mercy's sake,' I cried, feeling the left wheel of the vehicle already on the descent into the ditch.

" ' Drive to Tartarus and be quiet,' or something like it, was the kind and amiable response.

" I grew angry now, and tried the influence of abuse ; but nothing could move the obstinate madness of my Dutchman. ' I see the road plainly enough, don't be a fool,' and other such gentle phrases were all the reward that I got for my poor pains.   On urged the headlong Jehu, and not long deferred was our embrace of ' *mater et terra genitrix.*'   Down went our five hundred dollar mare, some eight or ten feet into the bottom of the ditch, and in a little brief moment were figured out a group of horse, and men, and buggy, precipitated, con-glomerated and accumulated, at sight of which Hogarth would have wept for joy.

" The violence of the fall stunned me for a minute.   When I came to myself, I was uncertain whether terrene habitations yet possessed me, or whether I was a groping ghost upon the banks of the dark Styx.   I listened for the noise of Ixion's wheel, and the rumbling of the stone of Sisyphus, but I heard instead the doctor cry out, ' d—— it,' as he turned over upon his side, in a mud-puddle by the head of our poor beast.   As-sured by this unequivocal evidence of vitality, I got upon my feet, and without waiting to make any inquiries about bones, I plunged through the rain to the house of our late host for relief.   I soon returned to the scene of distress with a lantern, and a sleepy negro.   Then, dear Angelo, there was a sight to look at.   O ! could you have seen B. come up to me, at that moment, with his pet cane, his unique, broken in his hands, with that wo-begone expression on his countenance—with that tragical attitude, hatless—his heavy eye-brow drip-ping with rain—his hair seeming to be in a state of liquidation, and fast flowing down upon the muddy adornments of coat and white—ah ! once white pantaloons ; his left hand point-

ing to the fragment in his right, as though that were the only
thing to be lamented or cared for ; while the mare lay groaning
in the ditch, and the lightning flashed, and the wind and rain
beat and whistled around us, and the negro yawned, and the
light of the lantern threw a narrow streak now upon one, and
then upon another feature of the scene ; now disclosing a hat
—or rather what had once been a hat—and now an umbrella,
and now a buggy-cushion. If your neck had been broken,
you would have laughed at this ludicrous piece of picturesque.
How can I give you an idea of the appearance of the hero of
the scene ? Think of old Lear, bare-headed in the tempest ;—
no, that's not it.   Think of Othello, in his bitterest anguish,
harrowing up his soul with the thoughts of what had been.
Do you remember Kean's air, and attitude, when he comes to
this melancholy passage—

> ——————————' Had it pleased heaven
> To try me with affliction, etc. *****
> *But there*, where I have garnered up my heart,
> Where either I must live, or bear no life.'

"I have given you brush, easel and canvas ; you have a good
fancy—draw the *waterscape* yourself.

"But be amazed at our escape. A broken dashboard, a
strained shoulder, and the doctor's ruined habiliments, made
the sum total of our added up distresses. I must confess for
myself some undefinable rheumatics ; but I am willing to bear
that infliction, by way of warning against rides by night, and
opinionated drivers."

MISCELLANIES.

MISCELLANIES.

RACHEL-BAKERISM.

I SHALL always believe, that people may be in the body, and out of the body, during the same moment of time. I am firmly persuaded, that the soul frequently quits the tenement to which it is assigned, and goes a-visiting other souls. Yes, and some times, it does not return. Under this theory, I account for the different characters and qualities of what are called strength of mind, genius, idiocy, and lunacy. When half a dozen good souls unite, and take up their lodging in one corpus, provided only the family regulations are discreet and are wisely administered, the union is strength, and the external man is esteemed a casket of intellect. If, however, too many, or too boisterous, or discordant spirits should hive upon one cranium, or if the domestic duties are not strictly enforced—Heaven pity the man—he is incurably mad.

I need not add, that when the soul totally vacates the premises, *Perditus* is esteemed a fool, and the devil institutes proceedings against him forthwith, under the absent and absconding debtor act. Short excursions, such as amorous exaltations, poetic flights, and all the variety of ruralizations, are the mere walks that the soul takes for exercise. These are the ordinary occupation, the daily going forth and incoming of the divine *afflatus* upon its peculiar and proper business.

But what a glorious exercise of divinity, what a blending of reality and imagination, of existence and annihilation, is

that power of the soul, which mingles the past, the present,
and the future! which makes even the gross body live back
in the young merriment of childhood, and taste by anticipation
the happiness of the far future! which makes the miserable
happy, the dumb eloquent, the sinner a saint! and is the
power controlled by circumstances? What have facts and
things to do with it? Rachel Baker had no education, but
when her body was asleep, her soul and *her soul's friends*
discoursed sacred music. What is a dream? a frolic, say
you of young Fancy, after old Judgment has gone to bed.
The substitute of imagination for fact—what is *fact?* How
do you determine any thing to be a fact? Do you not sometimes doubt whether you are not dreaming? Are you always
certain, when you dream? Have you not sometimes *dreamed*
you were *dreaming?* Metaphysicians and learned doctors
have discussed these matters with profound and ingenious
ability. But I must confess that I am not much enlightened
upon the subject, after all ; the many freaks of Alma have led
them all up and down and through the bogs and quagmires
of their art, just as did Trinculo the magic tabor of Ariel. I
have had myself a little experience in flights and absences,
and my irregular Jack-a-lanthorn spirit has beguiled me
more than once into a scrape. Of all these, hear one instance,
ye wise ones, ye custom house officers of reason,—ye measu-
rers and inspectors of the soul's exports and imports, and if
there be a philosophical explanation for it, pronounce, ex-
pound.

In the year 18— on the fourth of July, I left the burning
patriotism of my fellow citizens, and went a fishing upon the
classic waters of Communipaw. We watched in the distance the " tall spire and glittering roof and battlement, and
banners floating in the sunny air, and heard until nightfall,

the roar of the glad cannon. When the parade and bustle of the celebration were gone by, we headed our little row-boat towards Whitehall. It was a long and tedious pull, and my friend and I were juvenile in the exercise. At last our prow struck the wharf, and *terra firma* received us. I was worn out with heat and fatigue, and the excitement of our piscatory abductions. It was a long walk home, and I willingly accepted Horatio's invitation to stop at his domicil and rest. Scarcely had I set me down, when I found myself in the kingdom of Morpheus. I made myself happy there, until about eleven o'clock, when Horatio called me back, and advised me to go home, and to bed.——My father exacted of me good hours.——He awakened me, of this I am certain.——I rose, and directed my steps homeward. On my way, I had to pass the old family mansion, from which we had removed, some three years before. The street door was now open. The house—the wide hall—the entry lamp seemed all as usual. Without hesitation, and as a matter of course, and in honest joy, I entered, and closed the street door, wondering all the while why it should have been left open. I was wide awake, but I was living back in the third year previous. I was at my own home, as truly, as ever I had been in my whole life, and I was ready to give a good account of myself, for being out so late. On I passed—but nobody did I encounter. My foot was soon upon the stairs, and my hand upon the balustrade. Up I mounted into the third story, entered into my old room, shut the door, pulled of my coat, and turned to the bed, when, what was my surprise, to see in the dim moonlight sweetly sleeping there, a young lady ! She was beautiful—women sleeping in the moonbeams always are. My first impression was that there was some trick to be played

off upon me, by my cousin Harry, who had come from Scio to
spend the holidays with us.   I looked closer to see if it was not
a rag baby—when no ! Heavens ! she breathed—she moved
—Flesh and blood was in my bed ! I · dare not tell all the
rapid thoughts that burned their traces across my brain.—But
I do remember that among my better imaginings, I fancied it
possible that some visitors *might* have unexpectedly arrived, and
that my room had been appropriated for the accommodation of
one of them.   I looked around, and seeing a considerable
change in the arrangement of the furniture, my fancy became
almost conviction.   At all events, thought I, I must retreat.
With this intent, I took up my coat, and turned toward the door,
when horror ! the lady awaked, and screamed ! In ten seconds, a half drest, trembling boy burst through the door and
blubbered out " who are you ?"   I cannot tell which of us
was then the most frightened.   For my own part, I did not
know what to make of it.—" What do you want ?"—" who
are you ?"—" Mother ?"—came in quick succession upon my
doubting ears.   Rip Van Winkle was not worse off, when he
saw his own soul beating beneath the thorax of his progeny,
and stood the empty case of an absent spirit.   I was satisfied, however, that there was a mistake somewhere, and
I hurried to the door.

Down the stair way I rushed, but hardly had I reached the
landing in the second story, before I was surrounded by a
troup of old women.   That I was where I ought not to be,
was now evident ; and escape was impossible—and whether
I was in heaven, earth, or hell, I knew not.—" Who are
you ?"—" What are you doing here ?"—" What do you want ?"
screamed half a dozen shrill voices at once.—In that moment
I *died*.—I lived again.—" Go for a watchman, James," said

an old lady, in a low tone—aside. It did not escape me.—
Watchman!—thought I—thank God! then I am still in a civilized country! Happy institution of a watch district! "Ladies,"—I at last struggled out—"I have been committing
some egregious blunder—but what it is, I know not—I am a
respectable young man, I assure you—I had no sinister intentions in going up stairs—ask the young woman—nor am I
a thief—perhaps some of you may know my family, by repute. My name is Cypress—Jeremiah Cypress.—But I"—
here I was interrupted by the old landlady, who came forward
and exclaimed, "La! Mr. Cypress, is it you?—Why, to be
sure, I know you.—Why, I'm so sorry—but gracious—I was
so frightened—and here she told me her name, and I for the
first time found that she was the keeper of the aforesaid
boarding-house. It all flashed upon me at once—or rather,
I was back again into the year as numbered on the vulgar
calendar. "Dear madam," said I, "1 have not the pleasure
of your acquaintance, though I well know your name. I am
sure 1 can never sufficiently apologize for my rudeness. I
cannot tell how to account for it. But I have been out a-fish-
ing all day, and am returned very tired, and from not taking
particular notice, or from some distress or *absence of mind*, I
have followed a dream of former days, and"———"O" cried
the old lady, "you're very excusable, Mr. Cypress, it's fourth
of July, you know, and we all know, that"——"Pardon me,
madam—I assure you—I hope you don't think I've been
drinking—I have drank nothing to-day—that is, nothing of
any consequence"——"Certainly, Mr. C. I see you are not in
liquor, but"——"but my dear madam, I am not in the least affected—do not let me detain you, however, any longer—I
will bid you good evening, and do myself the honor of call-
8*

ing and making a further apology to-morrow."——" Good night, Mr. C. don't be distressed—it's fourth of July, you know—*I shan't say nothing.*"

Thus terminated this Rachel-bakerism excursion of my soul. I was very tired, but not asleep nor drunk—on my honor—and I do protest that the scream of that maiden banished every particle of fatigue, too, and well it might—for I hear it yet.

HYMN TUNES AND GRAVE-YARDS.

I WENT to church one night last week,

> "Ibam forte via sacra,"—

as Horace has it ; and into what shrine of shrines should my
sinful feet be led, but into the freshly hallowed tabernacle of
the new free Chapel.   It was Carnival week among the Pres-
byterians, the season of Calvinistic Pentecost ; and one of
the Missionary Societies in the celebration of its blessed triumphs, *bulged out*, on that night, from the windows of the
gigantic meeting-house, like the golden glories of thickly-
crowded wheat-sheafs from the granary of a heaven-prospered
garnerer.   Not, however, did the zeal of a Crusader against
the Paynim, nor the expected rehearsal of the victories of the
Christian soldier, draw me, unaccustomed, upon holy ground.
Wherefore did I, just now, pricked by conscience, stop short
in the middle of that line from Flaccus.   I could not add

> —"sicut meus est mos."

"*Meus mos*" stuck in my throat.   It was no good grace of
mine.   *Non nobis.*   Reader, I confess to thee that I was
charmed into the Tabernacle by a hymn tune.

Now, before I ask for absolution, let me declare, that my
late unfrequent visitation of the Church is to be attributed to
no lack of disposition for faithful duty, but to the new-fangled
notions and fashions of the elders and preachers, and to my
dislike for the new church music.

It had been an unhappy day with me.   My note lay over in
the Manhattan ; and I had ascertained that some "regulated"
suburban "building lots," which I had bought a few days before, unsight unseen, upon the assurance of a "truly sincere

friend," were lands covered with water, green mud, and black-berry bushes, in the bottom of a deep valley, untraversable and impenetrable as a Florida hammock.   Abstracted, in uncom-fortable meditation, I threaded my unconscious pathway home-ward, the jargon of the confused noises of Broadway falling upon my tympanum utterly unheard.   In this entranced con-dition, I came abreast of the steps of the covered entrance to the Tabernacle.   Here was done a work of speedy disen-chantment.   A strain of music came floating down the avenue. It was an old and fondly remembered hymn.   It was the fa-vorite tune of my boyhood.   It was the first tune I ever learned.   It was what I loved to sing with my old nurse and my little sisters, when I used to pray.   It was the tune that even now always makes my heart swell, and brings tears into my eyes.   It was OLD HUNDREDTH.

Fellow-sinner, peradventure, thou hast never sung Old Hundredth.   Thou wert not blessed with pious parents.   The star of the reformation hath not shone upon thee.   Thou hast not been moved and exalted by the solemn ecstasy of Martin Luther.   Perhaps thou hast had eunuchs and opera-singers to do thy vicarious devotions, in recitative, and elaborate can-tatas ; scaling Heaven by appoggiaturas upon the rungs of a metrical ladder.   Lay down this discourse.   Such as thou cannot—yet I bethink me now how I shall teach thee to com-prehend and feel.   Thou hast seen and heard Der Frieschutz ? I know that thou hast.   Be not ashamed to confess it before these good people.   They play it at the play-house, it is true ; but what of that ?   What else is it than a German Camp-meeting sermon set to music ?   It is a solemn drama, showing, terribly, the certain and awful fate of the wicked.   There is a single strain of an anthem in that operatic homily—worth all the rest of the piece ;—dost thou not remember the harmony of the early matin hymn unexpectedly springing from the choir in the neighboring village church, which, faintly beginning, swells upon your ear, and upon poor Caspar's too, pleading with his irresolute soul, just as the old head-ranger has almost persuaded the unhappy boy to renounce the Devil, and to become good? Dost thou not remember, as the tune grows upon his ear, the strong resolution suddenly taken, the subdued joy, the meek rapture that illumine the face of the penitent; and how, with head bowed down and humble feet, he follows his old friend to the fountain of pardon and to the altar of reconciliation? I see that thou rememberest, and—thou art moved; —"Be these tears wet?"

Here I am happy to receive the congratulations of the reader, that the similarity of Caspar's case and my own is at an end. Poetical justice required that Von Weber's Zamiel should carry off repenting Caspar from the very entrance to the sanctuary;—the civil sexton of the Tabernacle asked me to walk in, and showed me to a seat.

The hymn went up like the fragrance of a magnificent sacrifice. Every voice in that crowded house was uplifted, and swelled the choral harmony. The various parts fell into each other like mingling water, and made one magnificent stream of music; but yet you could recognize the constituent melodies of which the harmonious whole was made up; you could distinguish the deep voice of manhood, the shrill pipe of boys, and the confident treble of the maiden communicant,—all singing with earnestness and strength, and just as God and religion taught them to sing, directly from the heart. To me, one of the best recommendations of Old Hundredth is, that every Protestant knows it, and can sing it. You cannot sing it wrong. There is no fugue, nor *da capo*, nor place to rest and place to begin, nor place to shake, nor any other meretricious affectation about it. The most ingenious chorister—and the church is cursed with some who are skilful to a wonder in dampening people's piety, by tearing God's praises to tatters—cannot find a place in Old Hundredth where he can introduce a flourish or a shake. *Deo gratias* for the comfortable triumph over vain glory. It would be as easy for a schoolmaster to introduce a new letter into the alphabet ; and Old Hundredth may be said, in some sense, once to have been the alphabet of Christian psalmody. I remember a time when it was a sort of A B C for Protestant children learning to sing. It was the universal psalm of family worship. But its day has gone by. It is not a fashionable tune. You seldom hear it except in the country churches, and in those not noted for high-priced pews and " good society."

There is much solemn effect in the accompaniment of vocal music by a discreetly played organ ; but in my ears Old Hundreth suffers by the assistance. The hired organist and bellows blower, have each his quota of duty to perform, and they generally do it with so much zeal, that the more excellent music of the human voice is utterly drowned. And then there is a prelude, and a running up and down of keys, which takes off your attention, and makes you think of the flippancy of the player's fingers, and that your business is to listen and not to sing. No ; if you would hear, and sing Old Hundreth a-right, go into one of the Presbyterian meeting houses that has retained somewhat of the simplicity and humility of the early church ; or into the solemn aisles of the temples which the Creator hath builded in the woods for the methodists to go out and worship in. There you may enjoy the tune in its original, incorrupt excellence, and join in a universal song of devotion from the whole assembled people.

To Martin Luther is ascribed the honor of writing Old Hundredth. But the tune was older than he. It took its birth with the Christian church. It was born in the tone and inflection of voice with which the early Christians spoke their Saviour's praise. Martin Luther never did more than to catch the floating religion of the hymn, and write it in musical letters. It was such music that the poor of the world, out of whom the church was chosen, used to sing for their consolation amid the persecutions of their Pagan masters. It was such simple music that Paul and Silas sang, at midnight, in the prison-house. It was such that afterwards rang from crag to crag in the mountain fastnesses of Scotland, when the hunted Covenanters saluted the dawning Sabbath. Such simple music was heard at nightfall in the tents of the Christian soldiery, that prevailed, by the help of the God of battles, at Naseby and Marston Moor. Such sang our puritan fathers, when, in distress for their forlorn condition, they gave themselves, first to God and then to one another. Such sang they on the shore of Holland, when, with prayers and tears, their holy community divided itself, and when the first American pilgrims trod, with fearful feet, the deck of the precious-freighted May-flower.

> "Amidst the storm they sang,
>   And the stars heard and the sea !
> And the sounding aisles of the dim woods rang
>   To the anthem of the free !"

*   *   *   *   *   *   *

Where are all the old hymn tunes that the churches used to sing ? Where are " Majesty," and " Wells," and " Windham," and " Jordan," and " Devises," and other tunes,—not all great compositions, but dear to us because our fathers sang them ?

The old-fashioned church music has been pushed from its stool by two sets of innovators. First, from the rich, sleepy churches, it has been expelled by the choristers, who seem to prefer to set a tune which only themselves can warble, as if the better to show forth their clear *alto* voices and splendid power of execution. No objection is made to this monopoly of the musical part of the devotion of the congregations, for it is getting to be the fashion to believe that it is not polite to sing in church. Secondly, from the new-light conventicles, the expulsion has been effected by those reformers of the reformation, who have compelled Dr. Watts, not pious enough, forsooth, to stand aside for their own more spiritual performances. The old hymn tunes will not suit these precious compositions. But with genuine good taste in their adaptation of melodies to words, they have made a ludicrous enough collection of musical fancies, of all varieties, of tragedy and farce. Some of their ecstacies are intended to strike sinners down by wild hoopings copied from the incantations of Indian " medicine feasts," bringing present hell before the victim, and of which his frightened or crazed, but not converted nor convinced soul, has an antetaste in the howling of the discord. Of this sort of composition there is one which ought to be handed over to the Shaking Quakers to be sung with clapping of hands and dancing; I mean that abortion of some fanatic brain which is adapted to the horrid words of

> " O ! there will be wailing,
> Wailing, wailing, wailing,
> O ! there will be wailing ! &c.

Some preachers have thought it would be a good plan to circumvent the Devil by stealing some of his song tunes; as though profane music could win souls to love piety better than the hymns of the saints; and accordingly they have introduced into their flocks such melodies as " Auld Lang Syne," and " Home, sweet Home!" O ! could it be permitted to

John Robinson, the pastor of the New-England pilgrims ; to John Cotton, he who, in the language of his biographer, was " one of those olive trees which afford a singular measure of oil for the illumination of the Sanctuary"—to John Fisk, who for " twenty years did shine in the golden candlestick of Chelmsford"—to Brewster—to Mather—to any of those fathers of the American church, to revisit this world, what would they not lament of the descendants of the Pilgrims !

* * * * * *

I have conjured up spirits ! I am compelled, by an impulse which I cannot resist, to go on. I seem to hear some wailing ghost cry aloud—" There are more sorrowful changes in the body and spirit of the reformed church than in the fashion of the hymn tunes ! Where are the ministers of religion, who occupied the pulpits a few years since ? where are their churches ? where are the altars which our fathers builded, and where are the graves and bones of our fathers ?"

Alas ! poor ghost ! thou knowest not that " the age of bargaining is come," and that the Reformed church is a trafficker in the market, selling her sanctuaries for gold, and committing sacrilege for silver. The pious dead shall sleep no more in quiet graves. " *Requiescat in pace !*" shall henceforth be quoted in the price-current ! The departed brethren in communion, who were committed to the earth beneath the shadows of those sacred walls where first they knew the glad offices of the gospel, shall be turned out of their narrow tenements to make room for bankers and speculators ! Do I speak lies ? Go to the Wall-street church and get the flagrant proof. " It smells to Heaven !" That christian church draws a revenue from suits of offices for trade and barter which she has erected upon the graves of her children ; and brokers and attorneys—how can I speak it—find

the way to the temple of a heathen goddess,—not the altar of
Fortune nor the temple of Fame,—paved with old grave-yard
stones of the members of a christian congregation ?

Dr. Romeyn ! come not back to look for thy church in Cedar
Street ! It is clean gone. The merchants, who bought it,
bade a liberal price. They sing no hymn tunes there now.
The ground is consecrated to cotton, coffee, and dry goods.
The congregation have gone up town and built a splendid
cathedral. Go thou there, and see how glorious be the scar-
let, and gilt, and fine chased work of this reformed church.
But tell that minister to doff his humble suit of black. It
accords not with his pulpit. See ! looks he not like a beetle
in a gold snuff box ?

McLeod ! departed thunderer against the Pope, sleep on !

" Sleep on, nor from thy cerements burst."

Hear not the whispered horror. There are pictures hung
up behind thine ancient altar—and candles are burned there in
the day-time,—and strange tunes are played upon an organ
—and Latin is chanted there—and a silver bell is tinkled—
and frankincense is burned before the people ; but there is
not a bible nor a Scotch hymn book in the church ! and the
people do not sing, but they cross themselves ! Sleep on,—
sleep on, sweet shade ; too happy to have bee ncalled away !*

Garden Street Church is a heap of burned ruins. But the
number of building lots has been counted, and the elders
already feel the price within their grasp, and the name shall
no longer be " Garden Street Church," but " Exchange Place
Hotel !"

The Old Middle Dutch yet stands. O, may not that church

---

* It ought to be said, in justice to this church, that the sale of their old
meeting-house is to be lamented *with* them as a necessity, and not
to be charged *against* them as an offence. They were *driven* to a sale
by the result of a chancery suit, which imposed upon them the payment
of large sums of money, and they could not pick their purchasers.

be spared! May there not remain one unviolated tabernacle in this part of the city; if for nothing else than to remind us that there were Christians here in old times, and out of respect and regard for the memory of our forefathers?

The Brick Church.—I wish that I might be spared this task. But I cannot—I cannot forget that they, too, have agreed to sell their church and grave-yard,—to be used for a public post office—and that a decree has gone forth that the officers of the customs shall sit in the vault of my grandmother! The city corporation have absolved the trustees from their contract with them perpetually to keep sacred the land for a burial-ground. But have the people been released from their covenant to God, to respect the sepulchres of their brethren? Who has given them a dispensation to break open the cave of Macpelah? Or is there no moral or religious obligation—

"These bones from insult to protect?"

Is the word "sacrilege" abolished from our language?

But to what plea does this church fly for excuse? Can she complain that she is crowded out by the storehouses of trade and commerce, and that her people live so far off that they cannot walk to meeting? No, no. The brick church stands exactly where it should,—in the centre of the city—near the halls of Justice—on the public park; and it is isolated, and occupies an entire block, having no next door neighbors to annoy it or to hide it. Its familiar steeple towers where strangers and sojourners will naturally see it, and it is in the way of such as may inquire, "Where is a Presbyterian church?" The temples of God ought to be built in public places. They should not be hid behind dwelling-houses, like Chatham Chapel and the Tabernacle, nor in narrow lanes, like that one amid the pollution of Duane and Church streets.

Pull down the old Brick Church! That church known all over the christian world as a highly favored church,—a

church of eminent graces ! It would be a fit work for the
infidels who razed Jerusalem—and to disturb the grave-yard—
the proper office of hyenas ! O ! if the bond be not sealed,
if the bargain be not irrevocably concluded, let the church
save herself from the sin of this eternal condemnation.   Let
her send back the wretched pieces of silver !

   Tears—tears—tears !—I fear I have said too much.

   "And all this bold wrath comes out of a dissertation on
hymn tunes !" I think I hear my reader say.   And I see
some austere person rising and preparing to censure the
plainness of my speech to the churches.   He is learned, and
well armed with all sorts of weapons of argument.   He
comes at me first in Latin, quoting Terence :

> " Nonne id flagitium est, te aliis consilium dare
>   Foris sapere, tibi non posse te auxiliarer ?"

which being interpreted freely, means, " is not this a flagi-
tious piece of impudence in an unknown layman like you
to get up in the synagogue and lecture the elders,—to be wise
and pious about other people's crimes, while by your own
confession you are an unannointed reprobate ?"   Spare me,
spare me—most merciful inquisitor.   I waited until all those
who had a right to speak before me, might speak ; but they
were silent.   I felt it my duty then to disburthen my heart.
Sinner as I am, I do yet take deep interest in the welfare
and honor of the reformed republican church.   I am a descendant of the pilgrims, and it is not I, but their blood, that
speaks.   The cause is the cause of patriotism as well as
piety.   With one of the departed saints I feel and say,—and
I commend this as part of his testament,—to those who are
trying to improve upon God's institutions, " I shall count
my country lost, in the loss of the primitive principles, and
the primitive practices, upon which it was first established."

A WARNING VOICE AGAINST FAS-CINATION.

PHILOMATHES. What can be the reason that there are twenty women given to that craft where there is one man ?

EPISTEMON. The reason is easie, for as that sexe is frailer than man is, so it is easier to be entrapped into these gross snares of the deuil, as was once well proved to be trew, by the serpent's deceiving Eua at the beginning, which makes him the homelier with that sexe sensine.

"Dæmonologie" by "the most high and mightie Prince James, by the grace of God, king, &c.

JULIET. If they do see thee they will murder thee.

ROMEO. Alack ! There lies more peril in thine eye, than twenty of their swords.

ONE of the earliest victims of the too much indulged crime, whose character and consequences are the subject of the present discourse, was Patience Delight, a young witch of Franklin, Massachusetts. As her case is pregnant with good caution, and pertinent to the matter in hand, we will premise our observations with a brief statement of her trial. The account is taken from the original manuscript in the handwriting of the venerable Precious Smith, one of the early settlers in Smith's patent, L. I. and Chairman of the board of Commissioners on the occasion of this memorable investigation. The interesting document is preserved in the library of the Syrian Institute of Christian Hook, Matowacs, N. Y. The records runs, as follows :—

"A trew account of the triall of Patience Delight, &c. May 24, 1692. This being the day sette apart for the triall of that atrocious leaguer with Sathan, I tuck brother Condemned Fish, and Rev. Remember-Lots-wife Parkensen to sit with me in judgment, we being thereto specially commissioned. Opened court in the meet'n house with prayer.

9*

The pris'ner was brought in by the sherif thickly vailed, so that Sathan might not prevail upon the court thro' her devilish eyes, and with her arms straitly chained.   Then brother Per-severe-to-the-end Havery testified after this wise.   I was up into my broad-hollow wood-lot, cloast by Goody Delight's, mother of pris'ner, chop'n wood   Just towards the night, I felled a hickory, and sat thereon, resting and meditating. Then comes a certain rustlin in the bushes hard by, and turn-ing my head, lo! I see, thorow the tanglements, two sharp piercing eyes that overcame me with strange dread.   I thought first, it should be a wild catte, or a painter, the sharpness thereof was so severe.   But reach'n for my axe, and rising up, I see pris'ner pluck'n berries.   She looked at me again, and then looks away, and thereupon was I seized with unaccountable desire to keep looking at her, and could, in nowise, keep my eyes off her.   Which the tempter seeing and waxing bold, she saieth good evenen to me with much sweetness of voice that ran like tingling oil of Egypt thorow my marrow.   She keeps pick'n, and look'n, and shuten into my body the most distrustful contagion, insomuch that I was near beside myself.   Presentlie, on pretense of pluck'n beries, she cometh to where I sat, still shutin at me with her eyes, and when she comes cloast by me, restraining grace was utterly banished out of me, and I was wholly possessed with the Deuil.   Hearken not to my weaknesse, but to the power of sin.   Then, saied I. " Patience, how old art thou ? And she answered and saied " Sixteen years, and nine months, worthy sir."   Then Sathan takes my hand, and makes me to lay hold on her, and draw her to sette by my side.   She struggles, and makes outcrie, and saies she, " the man is be-witched."   " Yes," saies I, " and thou art the witch that hath bewitched me, and thou shalt cure thine own poisson."

Whereupon, she uplifts violent clamour, and I know not what else goes on, until my brother Condemned Fish, passing by, comes up, and clappes me on the sholderre, saying ' Hallo ! brother Havery ! what's the matter ?' And at that touch of that holy man, Sathan departed out of me, strait-way."

  " Sworn in open Court this 24 May, 1692.
      " *Signed*, Persevere-to-the-end Havery.
  " Precious Smith, *Head Deputie.*

  " The young men *Barnabas Ware*, *Boaz Daniels*, and *Walk-meekly Smith*, severally testify that pris'ner hath fascinated them at sundry times and in diuers manners. Saied *Barnabas* saieth, last Sunday two weeks ago, he couldn't keep his eyes off pris'ner all meetin time. Said *Boaz* saieth, for several months he hath been constrained, in spite of all he could do, when he went into meetin to look for pris'ner, and that alwaies a look from her went thorow him, and filled him with very dredful tremulation. That the fascination was painefull, but, natheless full of delight. Witness saith it was like the prickin of pins all over him, but when he searched, there was none to be seen. *Walk-meekly Smith* saieth that he went to home with pris'ner from singin schoole two weekes agoe. That he did so because he was thereto fascinated, and she moued him by her behauior so to do, having sat by his side in schoole and singin out of his booke, and that he had neuer done the like before, being a youth, aged only nineteene yeares, and subject to his father. That there was nothing in pris'ner's walk and maner that night, which might show forth the presence of the deuil ; only the cunninge puttinge on of modestie, and lookin strange sorts of earnest looks thorow her eye-lashes bent down, and, as it were, resting on her cheeks, which were seemingly all in a glow

of deuilish fire.   But next day and euer since witness hath
been sore distressed with losse of appetite, and melancholie,
and constant desire to be in companie with pris'ner, but is
afraid to touch her.   And he swears, before God, she hath
bewitched him."
    Sworn &c.   Signed, &c.

    "*Ruth Daniels* being sworn, testifies that she knows that
pris'ner hath bewitched Walk-meekly Smith, for that he now
shunnes witness, whereas he used to be familiar and good
friends, being witness' third cousin. . That last Sabbath week,
in the meetin, pris'ner tried to fascinate witness.   Witness
looked at pris'ner, to rebuke her for not minding to the discourse.   Prisner turned up her nose, and gave her such a
fierce look, that witness was fascinated to take up the hymn-
book, and was near about to throw it at pris'ner's head.
    "Hereupon, brother Condemned Fish saieth he remembereth
the witness uplifting the book, and how he checked her, and
he asks " is not this enough ?   Shall we not suddenly seize
defendant and cast out the curse from among us ?"
    "Then up starts.pris'ner, and throws the veil from off her
head, with incredible diligence and fury, and cries to the jury,
" Worthy sirs, take heed how ye give trust to false counselle,
and be not swift to stain your skirts with guiltless blood.   I
proteste to the Lorde I am innocent in this thinge.   Would
you put to death Susannah, and justifie the lying elders ?"—
with more of such bold assurance.
    "Hereupon it was plaine to see how Sathan struggled
in her ; so that Mr. Fish goes up and spat in her face,
and charged him to come out of her, and covered up her head.
Their judgment being passed, the people took her to a convenient tree hard by, and burned her with fire, while we all

exalted a song of triumph which well nigh drowned the cry of Beelzebub yelling with her voice."

The foregoing, was, probably, one of the most clearly established cases of witchcraft, which ever came into the condemnation of the judgment halls of New England. Yet, it is greatly remarkable, that this is the only authentic record of the kind. The adjudications in the Massachusetts reports are, generally, upon prosecutions against ancient hags, for sticking pins into little children, and committing other absurd outrages against the peace of the people, and the dignity of the church, and which made them, rather subjects for laughter at the oddity of their devil-play, than of fear for the substantial damages of their sorcery. Not another reported case exists of the flagrant basiliskism of the young witches who drew men, by their eyes, to run after them, and so lead them to melancholy ruin.

How clearly manifest in this matter, is the trickey cloven foot of the father of all witches !—Who prompts his favorites to anticipate a charge against themselves, by commencing a crimination of others !—The Pilgrim people, with whom Satan pretended to pitch his tent, were generally married women or antique. The complainants and witnesses were, almost invariably, young, plump, juvenals. So it came to be generally believed that a certain number of years were needful to a lady to be deemed worthy of supernatural visitations ; and thus, the fiercest witches in the land escaped suspicion. Many, doubtless, vehement fascinatrixes, of middle age, suffered just judgment, but it is equally certain that many innocent old ladies were victimized for simply wearing spectacles. That the grand juries began to ignore bills of indictment, was more owing to the fear of depopulating the country of their grandmothers, than to any new light of revelation shed upon

them by the judges. It was the fear of being compelled to
go without woollen stockings, that gradually brought the pilgrims to their senses. The approach of a hard winter un-
ravelled the yarn of witchcraft, and opened the eyes of the
boys of the Bay State. Time and cold weather pointed them
to comfort and safety. Then Connecticut set a good example
and passed its memorable statutes against young women.
Then Mr. Hutchinson got bold, and made his famous speech
at the clam frolic at Taunton. "If we continue these anni-
hilating executions," says he, "what an expurgated edition
of humanity shall be presented! If my aunts,—I have nine
—escape to the mountains, and then be caught, I shall see
them exhibited as monstrosities in the Zoological Institute!"

It becomes us to consider the errors of our fathers, and to
learn wisdom from their unwitting sinfulness. Much did
they lament. Much penitential sorrow did they pour out,
when they finally discovered that the witchcraft which afflicted the land was only the eyey galvanism of juvenile
blood :* Let the evil they did be interred with their bones.
They did all they could, for atonement, by expunging† the

* Is it not somewhat strange, that the principal sufferers as "weird
women," were "withered crones," when our fathers had before them this
testimony of the learned King James, concerning the Scotch witches?
"Many of them that are convict, or confessors of witchcraft, are rich, and
worldly wise, some of them fat, or corpulent in their bodies, and most of
them given over to the pleasures of the flesh, continual hauntinge of companie, and all kindes of merrinesse." *Demonologie, Book II.* If this case
can be, as it ought to be, taken as good evidence, the manager of the
theatre, when he next gets up Macbeth, ought by way of variety, to strike
out the "infernal, midnight hags," and put in something good looking,
fat, and funny.

† It is worthy of note, as a matter of history, that the first case of "ex-
punging" did not occur in our own time. The moral obligation of the duty,
as well as the clearness of the power, to "expunge," was felt in the case
of the Salem witches. So early as March, 1712, after the witch panic
had gone by, the church, which was then the state represented, met to

records of criminality they had made up.   Poor repentance, perhaps.   But the best they could offer.   Forgive them. " Blot out" was written on the tear that immortalized Sterne's accusing angel.

If history has taught us any thing, it has inculcated the good sense of the caution of Dr. Drake :—

" Trust not the evils of a woman's eye.—"

consider the case of Rebecca Nurse, who had been not only hung, but even ex-communicated.   The following notes are taken from " Upham's lectures on witchcraft."   Her case is first stated, as follows, page 90.— " Rebecca Nurse, the person whom the jury in the first instance acquitted, but were afterwards induced by the strong disapprobation and rebukes of the judges to condemn, was a member of the first church.   On the communion day that intervened between her conviction and execution, Mr. Noyes procured a vote of excommunication to be passed against her.   In the afternoon of the same day, the poor old woman was carried to " the great and spacious meeting house," in chains, and then, in the presence of a vast assembly, Mr. Noyes proclaimed her expulsion from the church, pronounced the sentence of eternal death upon her, formally delivered her over to Satan, and consigned her to the flames of hell."

Now for the redeeming record of common sense. look to page 123. " The first church, which had anathematised Rebecca Nurse and others, after their conviction, and previous to their execution, did all that they could by way of reparation.   It endeavored to erase the ignominy it had cast upon them, by publicly repealing and reversing its censures, and by recording the following affecting acknowledgment of its error.

" March 2d. 1712.—After the sacrament a meeting was appointed to be at the teacher's house, at two o'clock in the afternoon, on the sixth of the month, being Thursday ; on which day accordingly, March 6th, they met to consider of the several particulars propounded to them by the teacher : viz.—1st. Whether the record of the excommunications of our sister Nurse, —all things considered,—may not be erased and blotted out.   The result of which consideration was, that whereas on the third of July 1692, it was proposed by the elders, and consented to by an unanimous vote of the church, that our sister Nurse should be excommunicated, she being convicted of witchcraft by the court—and she was accordingly excommunicated.   Since which the general court have taken off the attainder, and the testimony on which she was convicted not being so satisfactory to ourselves, as it was generally in *that hour of darkness and temptation*,— this church having the matter seriously proposed and having seriously considered it, *doth consent that the record of our sister Nurse's excommunication be accordingly erased and blotted out, that it may be no longer a reproach to her memory and an occasion of grief to her children.*"

Doctor Cotton Mather found out that witchcraft lay in some-thing else than astrology, and divination, and conjuring and burning pictures, and gathering cabbages on All-hallow-eve, and putting chicken breast bones over the door-top, when he quoted in reference to his seven sons, all bewitched by the same young woman, a " member of his congregation," the pathetic lines of Virgil :—

" Nescio quis teneros oculus mihi fascinat agnos."

Tender lambs, indeed.—Poor devils.—All in love with the same, Syren! Burned, withered, blasted, by an opthalmic *coup de solicl !* Perhaps, all struck down at one shot from the same electrical battery! Well, let us reject all vulgar magic, all spells, incantations, charms. We are reason proof against them. But fascination we confess. Palmistry thrills ; but oculation sets the heart on fire.

Does any one doubt that a woman's eye is the fountain of witchcraft? Why, all history, all philosphy, all morals, all immorals, all experience, all nature, are full, fierce, and flash-ing with the proof.

History. Rise, witches, rise. Take them as they come.—Helen, Fulvia, Medea.—She boiled her father-in-law, and several other old gentlemen. She was a cook as well as a witch.—Sappho, Catharine of Russia, Rahab, Kitty Fis-cher, Joan of Naples, Joan of Arc, Paulina Buonaparte, Cleopatra, Lais, Thais, Tamar, Queen Christina, Judith, Xantippe, Delilah, Dejanira, Nell Gwinn, Euriphile Clytem-nestra, Dido —We will see no more.—Was there no witch-craft in these women's eyes ? It would be interesting to hear the ghosts of Alexander, Socrates, and Samson testify to that point before a committee of the House authorized to send for persons and papers.

The philosophy of fascination is full of attractive, and incomprehensible wonder. We feel it, and acknowledge its power, but we cannot define it. It does not belong to the exact sciences, but is rather referable to the metaphysical deportment of all-overishness. We can analyze the elements of ice, and give learned reasons why the blast that blows over us is hot ; but no man hath yet been able to resolve the agonies of the fierce and languid rays of woman's eye light. Some philosophers, who though good enough christians on other points, are well nigh materialists here, talk of "the subtle and active exhalation, or rarefaction of the humors of the eye," and of "the vibration of the nervous juices," and other such abstract imaginations, with a sort of familiar impudence, as if they had conquered the kingdom of darkness, and could put you up a bottle of fascination to order, at a moment's notice. But admitting these people, profane, to be correct ; they only show the *modus operandi*,—the means used for the expulsion and instillation of the invisible essence. They simply point out the lightning rod by which the fluid is conducted. The character of the element remains undeveloped. We are not certified whether it truly be Satan that sends it out in streaks. We are not assured whether it was a deception of our vision, when we have sometimes thought we saw the Devil in a woman's eye. Fascination is still in the clouds of chaos, with galvanism, and magnetism, and chemical affinities, and aurora borealises, and the music of the spheres, and the soul of the world, and all mysteries.

There be some men, who think themselves to be wise, that deny the existence of the element of fascination, and upon whom the eye of a beautiful witch falls powerlessly as upon a brazen statue. Such were never created out of flesh and blood, but were, in a hard laboring hour of some modern Prometheus, manufactured out of whitleather and red ink. If they do possess the attributes of humanity, perhaps, they can reason, if they cannot feel. We pray them, then, to be profound, and resolve us the well attested miracles of the Basilisk, and Opoblepha,—respectable brutes, who kill and cook their enemies and food, by staring at them. What is the power that enables the rattle-snake to draw by the invisible cords of his brilliant eyes, the shivering victim of his fascination? Why crouches the trembling quail under the steady eye of the pointer?

O! how we should delight to put one of these vain boasters under the magnetic influence of a pair of eyes we wot of! Thine, Julia, thine. Speak but say nothing. Let thine eye discourse*. Be first downcast, then inquiring and docile, then dignified, then tender, then earnest, then gently rebuking, all with thine eyes, thy tongue ever silent, and shortly thou wilt have a raging heathen in thy net, and thou shalt sing the song of the triumphant Maimuna.

> "I thank thee, I thank thee, Hodeirah's son!
> I thank thee for doing what can't be undone,
> For binding thyself in the chain I have spun!
>   The web is spun,
>   The prize is won,
>   The work is done,
> For I have made captive Hodeirah's son."

The power of Fascination rarely deserts the sex, even in extreme old age. Its character and quality are only modified. In youth, it is a consuming conflagration,—a persuading delusion,—a bewildering deliciousness,—a feverish rapture. The victims operated upon are boys grown up, and pensive. contemplative gentlemen. In senile years the element becomes weak. It degenerates into a venomous pestilence, that falls powerless upon men, but with considerable fatality

---

* ROMEO. She speaks yet says nothing—what of that?
     Her eye discourses.

upon little children, and cattle. Some writers, however, think that the spirit exists in the greatest quantity, and strength in gray antiquity. This notion, as we have seen, was the received belief among our forefathers of New England. Thus, one of the most eminent and zealous expounders of the craft says " Old bilious persons are most supposed to have the faculty, the nervous juice in them being depraved and irritated by a vicious habit of living, so as to make it more pestilent and malignant ; and young persons,—children and girls,—are most affected by it, because their pores are patent, their juices incoherent, and their fibres delicate and susceptible." Doubtless, the antique sybils are best entitled to the reputation of having what is commonly called " an evil eye," so far as concerns the laming of horses, and frightening juvenals out of their wits. They can " eyebite,"—as Cotgrave calls it,—sucklings. They may stare a cow out of her life estate.— They know how Φασι καινειν—to kill with their ugly " mugs" like the Haridans among the Triballians, and Illyrians, touching whom we have the certificates of Vossius and Pliny. But theirs is not the eye that strikes down and demolishes a man. The full glory of sorcery flashes from the οφθαλμος βασκαμος —the kissing witchery of the eye of twenty-five, and from the venefic Vesuvius of thirty.

The question as to the morality of Fascination, depends, very much, upon the discoveries yet to be made in its philosophy. One thing will not fail to strike the careful investigator. Mankind, from the very beginning of time, has shown no disposition to avoid the arrows which send poison through his veins, but has courted and rushed upon the dangers of the priestesses of the craft. It seems to be a part of human nature, to love to

" Bask in the beam of a dark rolling eye."

Hence have arisen all the factions of rhyme-grinders, jingling their bells, and laboriously whetting down their pewter
metal into edge no edge, " point no point," to the color of
some vixen's eyeball. The conclusion to be drawn from all this
mis-spent time, and painful elaborations of nonsense, is, that
Fascination is a sinful thing ; for it is not to be found recorded
in any book of trust-worthy authority, that humanity has a natural propensity for occupations which are good. Man is prone
to evil, and human nature is frail. Alas ! alas ! we are a
fearful race of reprobates, worshipping idols of flesh and blood,
and building us temples to sacrifice in, in the black eyes, and
in the blue eyes, and in the hazel eyes of witches !

We all have much, very much to answer for, touching the
empire of witchcraft. We have not resisted the Devil, and
made him flee from us ; but we have taken his arm, and
walked with him in company. How many witches' eyes
have stricken us with lightning, in our boyhood ! How many
enchantresses galvanize us, daily, with our perfect consent !
The sin is so pleasant, the indulgence so voluptuous, that we
drink it in like stolen waters. The Syrens adopt so many
shapes, and come in so many forms, too, that we dont know
it is a witch, until we "feel all over in one spot," as Dr. Ab-
ernethy happily expresses it. Nothing will save a man but
utter gynephobia. Some believe in spells. That was re-
puted a good charm composed by the learned friar Philomy-
glinus—friar of sins in public, and broiler of venison steaks
in private,—and which he wrote for King Arthur when he
started to travel in Circassia.

But it availeth not. Not Greek, nor Hebrew, nor High
Dutch, Amulet, Alexipharmic, nor Abracadabra, will assure a
man of safety. We have a Quaker friend, who wore a phy-
lactory of eel skin, around his right arm, for forty-five years,

and then finally caught the aconite from a fat widow of forty, that came to take tea with his sister.

A most confirmed witch, once, adopted the shape of a sweet saint, and pretended to try to convert us. O ! what beautiful tears, she shed, while she talked to us about the goodness of goodness ; and how through the liquid diamonds pendant from her eyelets, came the fierce mildness of her petitioning witchery ! Our heart was torn to pieces. ' Could we help loving her madly ? * * * * * That memory is painful —She afterwards bewitched a young minister, and carried him off to Oabu. That cured us.

We were once fascinated to go home with a young witch whom we met at camp meeting. How Satan can put on the appearance of an angel of light ! In that moonlit walk we were burned to cinders—O we were dust and ashes ! Our soul cried aloud, " it is good to be fascinated ! O keep on fascinating ! smile ! strike ! glory, glory, glory !" '

Why should we confess our sins to a public that is not apostolic ? The people shall not be our priest, and we will not kneel at their confessional. But we will listen to their *confiteor*, and give them good advice. Friends, study King James, live low, and wear green spectacles. Despair not because you are afflicted. It is good to be persecuted. Remember that—as his royal and pious majesty has told us— " there are three classes of people whom the Lord lets Satan buffet in this way ; First, the ungodly for their sins ; Secondly, the godly who are sleeping in their weaknesses and infirmities ; and Thirdly, the brightest saints that their patience may be tried before the world ;"—and again,—" No man is free from these devilish practices ; yet we ought not to fear, for we daily fight against the Devil in an hundred ways. So as a valiant captain dashing into the battle stays not his pur-

10*

pose by means of a rummishing shot of a cannon, nor the small clashing of a pistolet, so we ought to go boldly forward, and fight howsoever wounded."

This subject is not unworthy the serious consideration of congress.   Fascination is " practiced to such a great extent in this community," that it may yet be necessary to pass some conservative statute for its restraint.   Wont one of the parties take this subject up ?   They can make more out of it than they can out of " abolition," or any of the threadbare texts about " the bleeding constitution."   Here is a fearful crisis arrived !   We are on the brink of a gynecocracy ! women are travelling about the republic, preaching, lecturing, and uniting, fidelity, infidelity, and politics.   By the last census, it appears that they are multiplying and replenishing the republic in a most extravagant ratio beyond the sex that now scarcely retains the reins of government.   Our men are getting fast killed off by Indian wars and drinking.   Suppose it should so happen,—it might,—who can tell ?—that the next numeration should exhibit a balance sheet of seven women to one man ;—what will become of our liberties when the fearful fact is promulgated !   Let no confident youth think that this is the suggestion of a cowardly imagination, and that his personal safety would not be jeoparded by ambitious aspirants for queendoms.   We kneel even now to the tyrants, and hug the chains in which they bind us.   But once let Miss Martineau's horrible doctrines of the equal rights of woman be put into successful practice, and then good bye to purse and sword, and all !   We call them, now by affectation, the weaker vessel ; but it is in the multiplication table to make them vessels of wrath.   There were Amazons once.   Every one has heard of Boadicea and old queen Bess.   The word "heroine" is far from being a proper noun.   Is there not a prophecy on record, that a time shall come when seven women shall lay hold on one man?——Seven to one! We faint! Air, air! O! my country!

Yes, Congress ought to appoint a committee to inquire into the matter. Either side is interested to press the patriotic investigation. Here are substantial laurels to be won. Here may be built a name to last for ages. Let the self denying patriots of any faction raise a standard of resistance against witchcraft and petticoat government, and they will have a watchword and a battle-ensign, that would herald them to Victory.

AN UNPUBLISHED CHAPTER OF MRS. TROL-LOPE.

New York Judiciary—Politics—Specimen of a Chancellor—Water drink-ing—Dropsy—Church-yards.

THE most intricate and perplexing difficulty, after all, to be encountered by one going to America, to settle, who has been accustomed to a government of impartial laws, lies in the Yankee Judiciary Systems ; or as I would call them, machines for administering law. That of the state of New York, is the most democratic, as it is termed, and best illustrates to my notion, the worst evils of a republic. Mr. O'Flanagan, —the leading lawyer at the bar of that state,—furnished me with some facts, which, although I heard them with a holy horror, were related by him as establishing conclusively, the superlative excellence of their government. Their Judges and other officers of justice are not chosen at all in reference to their capacity, or experience, but simply in regard to their politics. The state I have before mentioned, is cut up into separate factions, which carry on a fierce and bloody warfare, for the purpose of getting possession of the offices of trust and profit. And my friend solemnly assured me that it was a universally admitted principle, that the only legitimate object of a republican government was the creation of offices for the people to fight for. These are called *the spoils of war*, and are distributed, with a sort of barbarian equity, among the soldiers of the successful party, as soon as the battle is over.

The most important and lucrative situations are generally gained by the best intriguers, and the leading chieftains.— They, on their part, have reciprocal duties to perform, and a solemn promise is exacted from them, when they are invested with their offices, that, after taking care of themselves, and their brothers, and uncles, and nephews, they will provide out of their power of patronage, for their partisan friends exclusively. A pregnant illustration of this rule appears in Noah's History of New York, in the case of one of the Chancellors of that state. The purport of the record is to this effect ;—That immediately upon the appointment being announced to the new incumbent—who was a country farmer—he took the boat for the city of New York, to comply with the "immemorial usages of the party ;" where, says the veracious Noah, "he hastened to smoke the calumet of peace with the grand Sachems, and hold a long talk by the council fires of St. Tammany." The meaning of all this is, that the new Chancellor, according to custom, treated his party to a sumptuous dinner.—It was paid for, I am told, by the Corporation of New York,—but he had the credit of it, —and he gave a public pledge, as to the course he would pursue. He appointed on the spot, two Sachems,—Black Hawk and Tecumseh,—to be masters in chancery, in the city of New York. In the course of the evening, the grand object of the assemblage was effected ; and upon this, Noah seems to dwell with great delight. I must quote him again—" and now came the time for the taking of the vows, and for the proof that the people had not been mistaken in their man.— Supported by William-s-co and Jack-targy, and six other chiefs, bearing bucks-tails, the noviciate arose under a canopy of Irish linen, bearing the motto 'Spolia Opima.' Nine cheers shook the vaulted roof of the venerable wigwam, while the signs of triumph were displayed. At length, the general voice of joy becoming husky, the new elect, laying hold of the ear of a half demolished cold pig, on the table, before him,—to signify thereby, that he would go the whole hog—pledged the toast, and vowed the vow, which binds us to him forever.   He swore to be ours, and ours alone. To take care of number one first, and then provide for his friends.   Nay, such was the generous and magnanimous feeling of the moment, that he drank ' Death to the man that won't take care of his friends, and decide their causes in their favor.' "

This Chancellor, I am informed by Mr. O'Flanagan, during his term of office, was true to his pledge.   He, immediately turned out of office all the Vice Chancellors, and Registers, and Clerks of the eight different Circuits of the state, and provided for eight of his brothers two of his brothers-in-law, three uncles, and an innumerable quantity of second cousins, and distant relatives in the country.— This was not all ; as my friend informed me ; for with judicious regard to a proper reward, for his kindness to his friends he went into partnership with all the new officers of his appointment and divided receipts with them.   That his new partners should not suffer by this encroachment, he added to the fees of their office, and required things to be done, which, O'Flanagan said needed not to have been done ; and to prevent complaint out of doors he reduced the fees of the solicitors and counsel of the court, in a correspondent ratio.   Of this Mr. O'F. complained bitterly, and said that the next thing he expected was that a rule would come out, requiring every lawyer who had a case, to go to the register, or assistant register, and give him a fee to draw his bill or answer.   These things, however, I do not well comprehend ; but they show plainly enough what republics are.   One thing, O'Flanagan told me, I think worth mentioning.   After all the people of the other party had been turned out, and their places supplied, there were seven men left unprovided for, to whom the new officer was deeply pledged. Having no other mode to reward them, he appointed them extra sergeants at arms, for the express purpose of bringing him water to drink, while engaged in Court. The joke of it is, that to keep them in employment, he was obliged to drink most lustily, and be taking potations during every moment of the day. It was one eternal sip, sip, sip. The lawyers looked on in amazement at the Tantalian rapacity of his thirst, and the Manhattan Company sent a petition to the legislature upon the subject. But the committee of the house to whom the matter was referred, were all of the Chancellor's party, and they reported that the imbibition complained of, was no more than was necessary in the officer who had the charge of all lunatics and poor widows with small children, and that the practice was commendable, since it kept constantly before the eyes of the bar, a glorious example of the preference of cold water, to brandy. Thus sustained, and the sign of Aquarius thus preferred, the Chancellor drank with redoubled zeal, and appointed two new deputy sergeants at arms. But alas! the aquatic influences at last overwhelmed him, and he finally died of the dropsy. I saw his tomb-stone, erected in St. Tammany's church-yard. On it is written a long eulogium, concluding with these words ; " Of him it may be truly said, that while he lived he was no ' small light,' and that he held his office ' dum bene, etiam optime, res pro se et suis gessit.' "*

* The constitutional term of his appointment to office.

AN UNPUBLISHED CHAPTER OF COL. HAMILTON.

[PICKED UP BY THE CHAMBERMAID, AT HIS LODGINGS.]

No intelligent traveller can fail to be struck on his arrival in this country, with the wretched condition of the lower order of the natives. The baleful effects of democracy can be read at once in their pale, emaciated countenances. Instead of the industry and honest ambition of European countries, their badge and brand is an indolent and thievish indigence. In no city in the world are there so many paupers as in New York. A stranger is constantly beset by them, and finds his own safety in the distribution of the contents of his purse. The precarious supplies obtained in this manner, support a large majority of the population. Great numbers of what are called the respectable classes, subsist entirely upon a kind of poor, small, yellow oysters, which are found in great abundance, at low water, upon a flat on the west side of the city, called the *Canal Street Plan*. I have seen thousands of people, men, women and children, floundering and flapping through the mud, on the Plan in the middle of the hottest days, toiling and sweating, and eating their truly republican dinners. Not unfrequently, more than one piscivorous gourmand dashes at the same shell-fish ; and then are enacted scenes that shock a civilized beholder. Oyster-knives and blood become well acquainted. It is not uncommon for hundreds of people to be murdered in one of these conflicts.

It is really refreshing, after witnessing these distressing evidences of the turbulent spirit of democracy, to turn to the contemplation of a people that has felt the happy influence of king and lords, game-laws, taxes and tithes. I often go down to the Liverpool packet ships, to relieve my disgust by a sight of something human. " Home, sweet home," rushes upon my memory, when I see these castles of the sea disembogue their freights of wholesome emigrants from the United Kingdoms. These hardy, enterprising, adventurous subjects of our glorious sovereign, are the only salt to be found on American earth. It is delightful to see them, as they stream along the wharves, dressed in their neat green frocks, white vests, and whole corduroy breeches, with a steadiness and solemnity which nothing could have taught but the influence of a sound government, and a bench of bishops. Immense sums of money are brought into the States by the emigrants ; and I was informed by Mr. Biddle the cashier of the National Republican Bank, that a greater revenue was drawn from the deposits made by these new comers than from any other source. From this class of individuals, too, have sprung all the distinguished men of the country. They are the only exception from the general charge of poverty and crime, which must be recorded against the United States. I have the best authority for this ; for the district attorney of New York told me, in confidence, that not a single individual of the three kingdoms had had a charge preferred against him, in the police office, for seven years and a half. These remarks cannot be applied to any other of the foreigners who flock to this land of liberties. Their condition is not much superior to that of the natives themselves. The Dutch and the Swiss struggle through a miserable existence, in New Jersey, and Pensylvania ; living principally upon cotton pods and the exterior filaments of the sugar cane, which these states produce in abundance. They are the mere helots of the Yankees in New England, who

VOL. II.—11

own all the southern and middle states, and who treat the wretched inhabitants with brutal tyranny. This very fully appears from the report of Captain Hayne, a member of congress from Florida, on bringing in a bill to provide for the sowing of grass in the streets of Charleston.

One caste of the indigenous population of the country, I ought, perhaps, to except from the general denunciation. I refer to the negroes, and to those who build their hopes of preferment here and hereafter upon their immediate emancipation from slavery. These elect people have come out from the common herd of their fellow citizens, and shaken off the dust of their feet against them. With a magnanimous disregard of means and consequences, they have determined that every bondman shall be free. No blow has yet been struck, but active preparations are on foot. Military academies and Sunday schools are extensively established among the free blacks, and the best poets and philosophers now living in the country, bear the sable hue of Africa. Major Jack Downing, who—as Colonel Lapis informed me—is an intimate friend and cabinet counsellor of the president, is an emancipated slave of John Randolph, the late catholic bishop of Massachusetts. The Jackson party, however, deny the friendship. A young lady in Vermont, of considerable accomplishment for a Yankee, has established a school of poetry and manners, for the good society portion of the negroes. This really "new academy" is watched with great jealousy by the government. The rabble have burned the school-house down no less than thirteen times, and the young lady herself is treated with all manner of indignity. She bears it all, however, with the spirit of a martyr; and so justly flattering to her is the notoriety she has acquired, that rumor speaks of a matrimonial contract soon to be consummated, which will certainly secure to her an everlasting reputation. These solitary instances of endeavors to improve the population of the country, are oases in this desert of selfishness and sloth. I visited the school in Vermont, in company with a distinguished philanthropist from New York, and was delighted with the arrangement and order of the establishment. The temperature of the school-room was rather too high, considering the number of the pupils ; but there was a peculiar aroma in the air,—which my companion told me was not to be snuffed but in the region of the Green Mountains—that made my two hours' stay exceedingly pleasant. What the result of all this will be, it is really fearful to anticipate. There will be bloodshed, no doubt ; but I cannot, as a man, refrain from going the whole length with my before-mentioned friend ; and with him, I hope soon to see the sons of Africa placed, in all respects, upon an equality with the whites— marrying their daughters, ruling in their councils, giving judgment in their courts, and feasting at their festive boards. Such millenial glories would, to be sure, be out of place in England, but in this boasted land of liberty and equality they would be appropriate and practically useful. Besides, as I have already intimated, all the brains in the country, with a few exceptions, are lodged in Ethiopian skulls.

I paid a visit, yesterday, to one of the courts, and witnessed a glorious manifestation of the fierce spirit of liberty. An action of assault and battery was on trial. The defendant was a tall, broad, raw-boned, big-whiskered individual, who had formerly been sheriff of Buffalo county. He came originally, from the city of Kentucky, and was born, I am told, upon one of the numerous sawyers on the Mississippi, where most of the families in that barbarous region reside. This was the thirty-seventh action against him, tried during this court ; and yet, notwithstanding he had knocked down two of the judges on the bench, and maimed all the constables but one, during this very term, not a single conviction could be had against him. His personal prowess made him invulnerable and irresponsible. When I entered the court room, I was startled by the unusual appearance of the forms of justice. Instead of the gravity of bag-wigs and hair-powder, and the grace of silk gowns, which adorn our king's bench, I found the judge dressed in a pea-jacket, with black stock, and pantaloons that might have once been white, and without a symptom of a shirt. The jury was drinking gin and smoking cigars, and the lawyers and the defendant were apparently preparing for a fight. Presently the judge got up, in a tremendous fury, and leaning over his desk, shook his fist at the combatants in the arena below him, and abusing the defendant in stentorian style, swore he'd "be——— if he'd stand it any longer !" No sooner was this done, than up rose a general cry of "make a ring, make a ring !" and the deed followed the word instantaneously. To my utter astonishment, the lawyers made a circle, and the judge pulling off his coat, leaped over the bar, and throttled his antagonist in a twinkling. The confusion and uproar were so appalling to me, that—not being accustomed to see fights in my own country—I am scarcely able to say what blows were struck, and what blood followed. After the lapse of five or ten minutes, I saw the judge again on the bench, and the defendant —who must have been worsted in the encounter—making a precatory speech to the court, gesticulating with his left hand, while with his right he endeavored to keep a dislodged eyeball in its socket. His discomfiture had a salutary effect upon the jury ; who, now that he was no longer an object of admiration or fear, gave a verdict against him for thirty thousand dollars.

CRIES OF NEW YORK.

AN UNPUBLISHED CHAPTER OF MRS. TROLLOPE.

PRIVATELY ADDRESSED TO THE PAINTER,

But intercepted and sent to the "Spirit of the Times" for exposure.

ONE of the most singular characteristics of this extraordinary race of semi-barbarians, after mentioning their horrid cannibal fashion of taking the shell off their eggs before they inthroat their contents, and buying tooth-brushes by wards—seventeen to a city of three hundred thousand mouths,—and hiring a Street Inspector to clean their teeth, once, every Fall and Spring, before "election day," is their "Cries." The most profitable book that Washington Irving ever wrote was entitled "Cries of New York." It was embellished with pictures,—which are very taking in America,—of a man crying "Clams! clams! Rockaway clams!" dragging along a spavined horse—no, hide, I should say,—spread over a lean hog,—for they have no *horses proper* in America;—an Irish Loafer—one of our countrymen, dear,—bawling "Vatermelings"—watermelons, my love;—a low Dutchman, with a two bushel basket on his shoulder, vociferating "'T-Oak"—tea-rusk, sweetest;—a mule, with a Yankee pulling him, and conclamating "Sand, sand, any sand!"—which last mentioned article is a great commodity in a country where they have no carpets. I am told that Johannes Jacobus Constellatio, the Rothschild of Columbia, made all his money by carrying around the streets rat skins, and crying "buy some beaver, Sir? Fresh from Oregon!"* Every thing here is done by crying. I got

* Vide Irving's "Virgil to Macenas"—"Sic iter ad *Astra*."
11*

out of the clutches of a gentleman the other day,—don't cry, kindest,—they called him " a police-officer," I believe, by mere vehement clamor.   It was something about one of the smallest silver spoons—you could take ninety like them in your mouth, and I only borrowed this single one to show the people in England how *little* things are in America.

Joy of my heart ! how I wish to see, to hold, to love you ! This brief bed-quilt of my soul will reach you per the British Queen Steamer in fourteen days.   For four nights, then, about that time, look upon the Moon, throw arrowy glances into her face :—she will feel the puncture, and laugh, and make her reflections on me.   So shall we meet, in spirit, animally magnetised.   I cannot be with you, bodily for some time to come.   I am taking lessons, from a Yankee Editor, in *Coolness*, *Sympathy* and *Gammon*.

I wish, my love, to call your particular attention to this system of " Cries."   A well got up pamphlet addressed to Lord Melbourne—say by " Anti-Radical,"—dont spell it *Aunty*,—might move great force for you, and I may yet see you in Parliament, the proud representative of the borough of Snake Hill.   Do try, dear !

The Worshipful Corporation of the City of New York have done wonderful work in this behalf.   They have established, and honorably maintain, schools for " Cries."   " Bellevue," " the Long Island Farms," and " the Egyptian Tombs," are the favorite colleges.   Private schools, under good protection, are plentiful.   But the birch-holder is chosen in reference to his strength of lungs.   To be able to " sing out," as they call it,—that is the great required qualification of a school-master. A boy, in this republic, has got his education when he can hurra, squeal, and scream at a political meeting, so as to be heard five miles off ;—not before that maturity.

For people not poor enough to go upon the town, and for that sort of democrats who advocate the honor of trade because they cannot get a dinner without it,—and I assure you, the country is full of such,—night meetings, *caucuses* they call them, or *carcases*,—are held. I was at one, night before last, drest in male attire, smuggled in by one of *your* friends, I can't tell you, now. Mercy! mercy! mercy!—the mixed up impudence, gin, patriotism and tobacco! Talk of the State of Maine—why, if those Orators had their prophecies fulfilled, not a single *estate* in England would *remain*, and Jack Cade would be made lawyer for the whole kingdom—Jack on both sides, or something worse. Nevertheless, it was pleasant to hear their sonorous throats rolling out " Hurra!" I confess I think that word far beyond our Parliamentary, shrill, argute " Hear," mixed up with the country and cockney discord of " Hee," and " Hea," and " E." The cry of " Hurra for Jackson!" made him President of the United States. It happened that the old man's message about the claims of the country on France, full of powder and ball, got out to Byzantium just before a young man named Stephens, who was returning from a mission to the Sultan of Petrea, started in a small privateer for New York. The lad opened, read, and explained the paper, and at the close, carried away by his enthusiasm, leaped up six feet, nine times, threw his cap on top of a five story brick house, and *cried* out what he called the old fashioned WAR CRY of " Hurra for Jackson!" That burst of soul, converted ten Arabs to Christianity on the spot. They immediately took berths in the forward cabin with John, crossed the Atlantic, got naturalized in the Marine Court, and voted the Loco-foco ticket. Their suffrages turned the election. Two of the Justices, I regret to hear, have since been " turned out." The Arabs said, on

hearing of this kick, " Allah is Mallah"—serves them right ;
—the rascally foreigners are bought over, and are owned by
the other party now.   Money and a popular CRY can do
any thing in this wild country.   They cry " Log Cabin," and
" Hard Cider," now, for General Harrison.   They *cry* " Cider," but they drink Rum.

You have heard much of American politics ; but you have
no conception of how much they do by cries.   The two parties which I call,—leaving adopted technicalities to the natives,—" Snug *in* office," and " Bleating *for* office,"—that's
the genius of this republic,—each train their young men, sons,
apprentices, and all, how to halloo.   For this purpose, they
establish schools which they call " General Committees of
young men," employ some forty-five-year-old.colt to sweat
himself down and look thin, to write their resolutions, and
copy extracts from speeches in Congress, and *seem* to be
youthful, and then to teach the real juvenals how to roar.
Such has been the crying up of this self-righteousness, and
crying down the iniquity of the candidates on the other side,
that several large gathering places have had their walls
cracked, and it is seriously feared by the mortgagees of the
" Masonic" and " Tammany" Halls that they will fall in and
smash the security furnished by the party speakers.   But I
never heard the watchword cry of battle more gloriful than in
" the Park."   There needed no torches, though they were
there, for the stars attended that meeting thick, and sang,
though I don't think those democrats heard them.   I did.
And when the boisterous ocean of *base* went up to the *treble*
of the blessed sky, after some humble flower-planter had sown
his seed, I heard, distinctly, the mingled chorus of seraphic
harps, hymning composite harmony with Loco-Foco shouts
of Hope.   O ! I am sorry you left this country so soon !   If

I only thought you was safe off the Newfoundland Banks! Don't stop to fish, dear—Codfish are coppery at this season of the year.

Hang politics! Let me simply speak of the music of the country, which the democrat simpletons call *Cries.* In doing this I do not mean to encroach upon the investments of Charles Horn, who has entered into great engagements to diapason and appogiature the street cries, and the yells of the suffering slaves as their mistresses beat their sculls in with the kitchen shovel ; nor to deprive the poor poets of Gotham of their glorious gathering up under the butchers' stalls in market, of things "long time ago." I speak from my own gathering.   *   *   *

But, for a simple, lone woman, to lie in bed and hear the glorious festivals of the early birds of New York! it is rapture to open your windows and let in the operatic sweetnesses. If I had musical talent I would save expense, and not trouble you ;—but you will have to engage Horn to furnish the music. I can give you only the words. E. G. " Hea!—s ! adishes ! —raydishers !—raydishus !—watermylions ! Harcoal !—charcoal ! Sawbries !—strawburruos !—sawbris ! Sun ! Morning Hayold !—Heruld ! *and Brother* Jonathin ! Ha-aiep ! yep ! hinc ! yop ! wick ! wo ! mil-ick !" Then right afterwards, " Butter-my-leg ! or buttermillock ! Journal of Commerce, ma'am ? *Here's* the Courier and Enquirer !" —The last two cries *sotto voce*, as those publishers stand upon their dignity, and employ boys who can whisper so as not to be heard above the noise of the steam they are letting loose from the delaying river-crafts.—Ba-a ! A-a-a-ah ! go the calves and lambs, half starved on a North River sloop close by. " Go 'board the Constitution, sir ?" cries a fellow in a boat, pulling out alongside. Next—" Passengers an't paid their passage please step to Cap'n's office and SETTLE!" On the wharf, again, a negro pokes you in the ribs, with, "Carriage, ma'am?"—— "Take your baggage?" cry out fifty licensed runaways, hired by the Corporation out of the House of Refuge—the only legitimate opera house in the city. Get into Broadway, and a Greenwich coach runs over you, while a Bowery omnibus heals your wounds with, "Bowery! right up! take a seat, ma'm!" while you are rolling in the mud. "Hot corn! ho-ut co-orn!" cries a muddy-faced Abyssinian, as she pokes into your amazed eye an ear of maize. "Hot corn, piping hot! come and buy my lillywhite corn and let me go home." —I particularly commend the last cry to your study before Horn & Co. get hold of it.—"Baked pears! baked pears!", chimes in an old wench, as she applies a pair each side of your nose. "Eysters! here's your fine fat eysters! Try one, ma'm." Then some tender urchin ushers out his democratic infidelity, and a third takes up the counter and screams at the top of his *alto, New Ery, Sir? New Ery, Sir?*" and seventy-ninthly chimes in some Conservative in base, jingling harsh discord, against whom all cry out, "Keep your Times, sir, keep your Times." "Any soap fat? any ashes?", cries a decent looking Yankee, who pretends to be an Irishman, so that he may have the liberty of the town, and can steal easily. His comrade at his side cries legitimate Tipperary, vociferating in tripple allegretto, "Onny sopfat on oshes?" "Toot! toot! toot!" goes a tin horn, while a little boy running along side of it cries, "Here's your fine fresh mackerel! —Toot! toot!—here they go-ey!" Then comes some sweet minstrelsy from the sweeps,—all beautifully black, and with the sweetest teeth, my love. I am told some of them are our own emancipated, from Jamaica. Such music as they have got! Such throat-rolls! Such eye-waves! It would be

impossible for any English woman to be here for a day without becoming an advocate of anti-slavery. Listen, and put it into poetry and sing it. " O ! o-o-o-o-oh ! O ! o-o-o-oh-oh ! O ! oh ! ohi, ohi ! oho !" It rolls from their angelic, sooty tapanities, which the people of the States vulgarly call " *lips*," with such a pleasant grace, that it always reminds me of the dying howl of my dear lap-dog Julio—whom you fed to death with too much toast,—crying for another bathe in the milkpot at breakfast.

I have not mentioned a tenth part of the parties in this opera—I have given you but some of the principal characters ; you must fill up the under-actors, supernumeraries' and spectators' names yourself. The Carnival in Rome, or in Venice, is a fool to it. People there *act*—here they *live* their parts. It is a chapter of their education and duty. Every crier must be appointed by a court ; auctioneers and masters in Chancery are nominated by the Governor, and elected by the Senate. Little-necked clam-boys are examined and certificated by Chief Chamberlain and Lord High Hospitaller Harry Van Cott, at the Golden City of Jim Acre. Few, I am told, pass the test ; the most being destined for weeks—Cale.—i. e. Calendar—to improve for their desired circuit. They get their throats in sweet order after this tuition, and can sing like gypseys. Sweet monkeys one got my cornelian off my finger Sunday afternoon, so innocently and full of play ! Poor thing, how sorry he was he couldn't find it on the carpet ! He was an English boy, my precious one, born on the passage, crying all the way ! Wasn't that funny ? But instinct taught his cry. His mother's thought at his conception taught him New York. Your natural shrewdness and good sense will readily find the reason why the Americans have succeeded so desperately in gorging our best mu-

sicians ; whistling down every bird in the British horizon to their mobocratic stools. *They love music, and they will have it.* They have a taste. They made Malibran, and gave her a husband and a name. Every raspberry girl from Bergen knows this, and when she pours out sound of "*rarseburies*" from her wide-startling lips, she is careful to stream from a deep-rushing throat, and to volume out the tone opposite the house of the Alderman of the district, and sell to him a penny a basket cheaper than to any of the commonalty. I *cry* you mercy for this long epistle.   Far, but faithful,
  Believe me, I think their *cries* " Macedonian,"
    Though beautiful to be *listened to, only,* your own
                                          TROLLOPE.

THREE HOURS WITH TIME.

IT was a sultry afternoon in the month of August. Clara was not, as I had hoped she would be, in her seat at church. My disappointment and a hearty dinner made me wish myself back at home ; and I beheld with dismay the Rev. Dr. Spintext, so celebrated for his acuteness in drawing distinctions, and for his ability in expounding mysteries, wipe away the perspiration with his blue cotton handkerchief, as he repeated for the third time, in a climacteric of emphasis, a text from the Apocrypha. A wicked, heathenish languor came over me ; my head was dropping upon the desk in front of me, when I felt my elbow slightly touched by some person in the aisle. I turned around, and observed a significant, queer-look-

ing old gentleman, in whose face was combined a singular appearance of youth and age. His face was wrinkled all over; yet the wrinkles were not the furrows of decay; each one was full of elasticity and life; and his eye, which was protected by long grey lashes, exhibited the buoyancy and good humor of youth. His person was enwrapped in a loose grey cloak, which effectually prevented a close scrutiny into the figure of the wearer. I had, however, no time for observation, for the old man, leaning over the pew door, immediately addressed me in a low voice, and asked,

"Will you step out with me one moment?"

I was heartily glad to get an excuse for leaving the theopolemic arena; and hoping that the congregation would think I was suddenly sent for on important business, I immediately unbuttoned the door, and followed the old man out of church. As we proceeded down the aisle, I observed that the doctor stopped, and the people stared, as if astounded at my irreverence; and all eyes were turned upon me. To my surprise not a creature looked at, or seemed even to observe the old man, who moved along as noiselessly and swiftly as a cloud. When we had at last fairly got out into the churchyard, and were alone, my new friend turned to me.

"You have no disposition, I perceive," said he, with a humorous yet courteous glance of his eye, "to stay and see that old screw-driver boring into non-essentials, and destroying bad instruments in trying to prove worse theories? Come, I have invited some friends of mine to a symposium with me to-day. You will be pleased with their acquaintance. You will go with me? Get on my back?"

This was all said sooner than I can repeat it, and the deed followed the invitation with infinite rapidity. Quicker than thought I found myself astride of the old gentleman's shoulders, and before I could recover breath, we were above the steeple of the church. As we began to ascend, my future host stretched out from underneath me a pair of huge black wings, with which he made the air to scream, as if severely wounded by the rapid strokes of their pinions. His old gray cloak floated off behind us, in the shape of a dark vapor, and was soon lost in ether. The rushing wind struck off a very genteel wig, with which his bald head had been protected; and my new friend, now stripped off his different masks and coverings, flew, confessed and proven to my astonished eyes, *old father Time.* There could be no illusion. There was his horrid scythe in one hand, and his hour-glass in the other, and his single gray forelock, floating in the wind; and certainly no genius nor devil could fly half so fast. Up, up we flew. What a situation for a poor sinner like me!

My health was not very good; and my friends had lately been telling me that my days were short, and that my *time* was passing fast away; but this was rather faster work than either my friends or myself expected to see going on. My whole life, and all the thoughts and feelings of my life, seemed centered in a single point. I thought of my many insults, neglects, and abuses of the old gentleman; and horror stupified me when I remembered that I had several times, tried even to kill him. "It is all over with me, now!" thought I: "this autocrat of the world, this ruiner of empires, this humbler of proud and wicked hearts, is about to take his swift revenge." My limbs relaxed, my muscles seemed to melt, when the old gentleman, turning his head partly round, spoke in a sharp tone,—as if to chide me for my want of confidence,—and bade me hold on tighter. I felt re-assured by his manner.

"You much mistake my character," said he; "you have

nothing to fear from me. I have read your thoughts and pity your feelings. I am not revengeful ; no man ever suffered ill from acquaintance with me, unless he abused my gifts. But I can't talk and fly well at the same time. I will converse with you more at freedom when we get to our journey's end. In the mean time carry my hour-glass, for I have got more than my usual load, and can scarce grasp all."

So saying, he reached me his glass, and I felt not more comforted by his words than by the view of sundry black bottles, nicely wired and waxed, which disclosed themselves to my eyes in his act of turning. I took courage and a firm seat at once. If I had been singing the third verse of " Away with melancholy" in mine own parlor, I could not have felt more easy and comfortable. Our conversation was momentary and monosyllabic, until I observed that we were descending over a sharp ledge of the Rocky Mountains. Here we laid on our wings, and soared along more leisurely, while old Time looked about, as if uncertain where to land. Occasionally he struck with his scythe at some projecting point or eminence, when instantly the face and surface of the mountain became changed. A single touch of that magic weapon wrought wonders as we passed along. A fertile plain would in a moment occupy the place of a barren ledge of rocks ; or a lake reflect back the clouds and the neighboring scenery, where just before some bleak Atlas had reared his head. While hovering about this region we had a very unembarrassed conversation upon the subject of the future destinies of this part of the world. The prospects of the Indians—the growth of the western states—the dissolution of the Union—these, and other topics of the same character, seemed to be familiar matters with my companion ; and I must say, that upon this occasion I gained some knowledge of Time's intentions, which certain great men would give all their present prospects to possess. But I need not say, perhaps, that as to my prospective information thus obtained, my mouth is sealed. At length we alighted upon a romantic lawn, which nature had made a garden after her own sweet simple fashion, where wild roses gave their sweets, and the honeysuckle encircled the untrimmed althea, receiving and breathing perfume. We directed our footsteps to a grove of venerable oaks, which spread their magnificent branches hard by.

"These oaks," said Time, "mortals would say have defied my power. But I feel pride in stating that they have been planted and nurtured and preserved by myself. Here is my favorite retreat. When sick of the abuses and unkindness of mankind, here I have often found the wished-for retreat of the philosopher of nature. How sweet retirement is, Mr. Cypress."

I was glad to find that the old gentleman was getting to be sentimental ; for the seclusion and sweetness of the spot had already made me rather lack-a-dasical. But suddenly checking himself,

"Here," said he, " I have invited my friends to meet me, I must apprise you who they are. You must not expect to find my equals ; I of course, have none. They are my dependent family connections. Spirits, like me ; all alike, and yet all different ; parts of me, yet distinct, and to a certain extent independent sovereigns ; not so old as I am, yet born at the same time. These are mysteries, I grant you, and you need not ask to understand them. My friends are the *Hours.* Not the sickly nymphs whom the mawkish fancy of the Grecian poet conjured up. No, my young friend, I know that it has been abusively said of me, more than once, that I occasionally am lazy, and borrow speed and swiftness from the

smiles of woman ; but I pledge you my word that these reports are only the base slanders of my enemies."

Here the old gentleman spoke with emphatic indignation,
and unconsciously striking his scythe against a huge rock,
upon which we were treading, there sprang up where the
blow was given a pure, bubbling spring of water. I smothered
an ill-restrained exclamation. The old gentleman took no
notice of the matter.

"Pardon my feelings," he continued, "I am getting old,
and perhaps peevish. My friends are twelve young gentlemen,—I say *young*, according to our mode of computation,—
hearty, hard-working, industrious, good fellows, who have
been fellow-laborers with me since I first followed my present business. You will find them agreeable if you choose to
have them so, or they will be cross and ill-natured, as you see
fit. They partake a great deal of the fashion of the times,
and are not unfrequently a little irregular ; but this, I assure
you, arises from nothing but their accommodating disposition.
Within that grotto, which you see upon your right, we sometimes meet, and talk over matters, leaving some one or more
of the twelve on the watch ; and if any thing goes wrong in
our absence, we rectify the error at the next leap year, or—if
that wont answer—we have a new calendar, or new style,
manufactured, to set things right again. But come, let us
go in."

So saying, we entered a spacious grotto, where I perceived
the company had already begun to assemble. I have read
of the cave in Antipharos ; of the heaped up treasures, and
kingly glories of the chambers of the east. I have seen in my
dreams the gorgeous magnificence of the palaces of Arabian
magi, but what, O Time, can compare with the spectacle which
now burst upon me ! Here was indeed the museum of ages.

12*

Antiquity, modern years, the four quarters of the world, might here have each claimed some precious curiosity. The crowns and sceptres of monarchs, the robes and stoles of orators, the gowns of philosophers, the cimiters of heroes, were here. The riches of the world, spiritual as well as physical, here met, and were apparent to the eye of sense; and I found that my heart was affected by their contemplation, with the same emotion—though to an intenser degree—which I have felt when reading what history has said of them. Here were embalmed and encased in ethereal adamant the faith and constancy of suffering martyrs, the tears of oppressed virtue, the fame of the conqueror, the pangs of the vanquished, the pride of the usurper, the aspirations of the poet. In fine,—for I cannot attempt even the heads of a catalogue of the collection,—here were the essences of all the virtues and vices, passions and emotions, glories and disgraces, which ever entered into the hearts of men, or marked their career, embodied and rendered palpable to vision. I had no opportunity for a close examination, although my curiosity drew me very powerfully towards an immense collection of books and manuscripts, over which was written in golden characters, "Alexandrian Library." I could barely make a few reflections, when my host, taking me by the arm, whispered in my ear, "Here are treasures which the world accuses me of having destroyed; bear witness how I am belied." We had entered so noiselessly that the Hours did not at first perceive our approach. They had all arrived except Twelve O'clock, and also except Four, Five, and Six O'clock, whom Time said he had directed to stay behind, and wait upon Dr. Spintext and his congregation. We concealed ourselves behind an ancient statue, while Time hastily sketched the characters of some of the guests. There was a strong family likeness between all of them, and all wore sharp, short wings. Each had a small sickle hanging at his back, under his wings, yet all were dressed differently, and were dissimilar in their conduct.

"That tall, lean, straight young man, standing by himself," said Time, "is One O'clock. He is the most unsociable of the whole family, and feels vain of his being number one. He has to work in the heat of the day, however, and you observe his retiring shirt collar and moistened kerchief give proof of his exertions. I often attribute his apparent melancholy to fatigue and exposure to the sun. He possesses some singular and *unique* qualities, and we are always happy to own him for *one* of us. Two O'clock stands a little on his right, with his back half turned towards us. He is as fat again as One O'clock, but I assure you not the less active. He eats a great deal, and yet is always hungry and full of business. He has lately got into the brokerage profession, and has almost as much to do with exchanging money and taking up notes as Three O'-clock, whom you see approaching him. I have expostulated with both of them against pursuing a profession for which they are certainly not so well qualified as Five, Six, or even Seven O'clock; but young men now-a-days, you know, will choose their professions for themselves. Seven O'clock is taking a seat there at the tomb of Thersites. I'll lay you a wager now that fellow's got his hour-glass filled with an infusion of tea, instead of sand. I am afraid, sir, that young man has acquired an affection for some old maid. He's become scandalous, and makes remarks upon his absent companions; but what is most suspicious, he will not drink wine. It will do your heart good presently to see him fill his glass half full, and when his health is proposed, sip it with a simper, like nothing temporal, I assure you. That fine looking fellow, combing his whiskers, and who looks as though he had just escaped from a frisseur's show-window, is Master Eight. He has many good qualities, sir, and possesses infinite versatility of talent. He has chosen, it seems, to-night to be tricked out for a ball, or an opera; and to carry his operations among the fair sex; not that he cares two-pence for them. By no means; the girls have laid a great many traps for him, particularly in the country; but they have found out, at last, that he was born too early in the evening for them. He is a literary and political character besides, and many a public meeting for charitable purposes has been held under his auspices. What I say of him now, Mr. Cypress, I may say of all of us. Though each has his own business to attend to, yet we all attend to each other's; we have to be like lawyers, ' *omni laudé cumulate*,' a sort of jack-of-all-trades people, learned in ' *omnibus rebus et quibusdam aliis*.' We have all manner of people to deal with. You will perceive, sir, by examining, closely, that Master Eight has a pack of cards sticking out of one pocket, and a camp-meeting hymn book out of the other. Whether piety or picking pockets employs his next moment depends mainly upon the character of the mortal he meets. Nine O'clock, whom you observe figuring about those mirrors, is nothing more nor less than Master Eight set in motion. He has not so much starch but more fire and vivacity; but when he chooses, he is insipid enough."

Here old Time gave a tremendous yawn.

" By my hour-glass," said he, " I never can look at that cross fellow with two heavy eyes, without getting sleepy."

I directed my gaze to the person who gave cause to this exclamation, and perceived a sleepy looking old fellow with a book in his hand, whom I took to be Ten O'clock. But that yawn had closed the lecture on heads. The whole company simultaneously started and rushed towards our covert. In the same breath we advanced upon the Hours, and answered all inquiries by timely gratulations and welcomes.

" My dearest friends," said the old gentleman, bowing with the grace and elegance of his most polished manner, " I am quite delighted to meet you all again. I trust I have not kept you long in suspense. At least, I hope you have made yourselves happy. Allow me to introduce to your acquaintance my friend Mr. Cypress. He is a very respectable mortal of good family—can get *tick* wherever he goes, and never suffers his clock *to strike the hours*. He has a friendship for us, gentlemen, and wishes to make the most of us."

Here I was almost crushed by the embraces of half-a-dozen of my new associates.

" But come, my friends to business. ' *Tempus fugit*,' is my motto you know. Be seated. I promised you last new-year's eve, you remember, to give you a taste of the new importation of Burgundy. I have secured the boys, and have them here."

As he said this we seated ourselves at a long table, and our host drew forth twelve veritable bottles of rich red Burgundy —*burning red*.

" Gentlemen," said he, " I will give you *my certificate* that these are the true, genuine boys ; ' *insignes pietate viros*,' as Virgil has it. But where did I get them ? you ask. Why in a very good place. The same spot where I picked up my friend Ascanius here. To make a long story short, the sexton's back was turned, I caught hold of my forelock, the bottles were under my arm, I touched Mr. Cypress's elbow, and we were here in no time—fill, gentlemen, fill—bumpers —your health—I am happy to see you all, at all hours."

" My dear Tempus," said Nine O'clock, " your spirits are as etherial as your wine. That ' iron tongue' of yours, as

Will Shakespeare used to call it, is as quick and voluble as the piston of the North America."

"Like causes produce like effects," said Seven O'clock, in a low tone. "They both are set a-going by *steam*."

"Not of the tea-kettle," said Nine.

"Nay, now, my friends, this is ill-timed for gentlemanly hours," interposed Time. "I hold that it is quite enough for us to be abused by our enemies; let us not suffer our keen wits to wage war either upon each other's spiritualities or temporalities. I, for my part, am sober and pious as the world goes, yet, although, I have kept pace with the improvements of different ages, and have accommodated myself to the different fashions of the day, yet I find that my enemies are universal. In attempting to please all, I have pleased none. Mankind, I find, have been determined to find fault with me ever since I had any thing to do with them. In every age I have been accused of being worse than ever I had been before, and of getting worse and worse every day. Is there a term of obloquy with which I have not been visited? Am I not reproached by all manner of cunningly devised phrases of the poets, and by down-right Billingsgate of the mob? Yes, gentlemen, and it is so with us all. We are, in the same breath, accounted swift and tedious, long and short, certain and unknown. '*Tempora mutantur*,' says the classic; 'the times are out of joint,' cries the poet; 'hard times, bad times, poor times, miserable times,' ejaculates the *canaille*. What are we not in the esteem and on the foul tongues of our malicious slanderers? Yet, we bring them daily good gifts, and many of them, particularly the political part of the world, are content to live and be waiters upon us. I sometimes seriously think of getting rid of the connection; but the moment that I hint an intention to move into another country, all the world weeps, and goes distracted at the thought. However, we must ' grin and bear it,' my friends, and in the mean time, *here's to better times*."

Here I ventured to remark, on the behalf of some of my earthly friends, that I thought the judgment of Time, although in general impartial and controlling, to be in this instance prejudiced and too indiscriminate.   I insisted that many mortals loved Time, and the things of Time. above all things ; and that for this very affection they suffered martyrdom every day.   I referred to the cases of newly married lovers, and people about to be hanged ; and was proceeding in my vindication with some zeal, when I was rather abruptly called to order by two or three of the company for " making a speech against time" as they called it, and was reminded that I was not in congress.   As I was attempting an explanation, we were interrupted by the approaching sound of some bacchanalian ditty outside the grotto.

"Twelve O'clock has not been at his studies to-night I opine," said Seven O'clock.   " When he arrives it is generally time for decent people to go home."

By these characteristic remarks I was prepared to see Master Twelve, who now staggered into the room, bowing and bending with the most ludicrous affectation of dignified politeness, and after divers circumgyrations, took his seat by One O'Clock. The appearance and conduct of this personage were rather disordered.   His face was pale and haggard—his eye dead drunk.   His clothes were cut after the newest pattern of modern grace, but exhibited unequivocal symptoms of having been in a recent fray.   A watchman's broken lanthorn supplied the place of his hour-glass, and the bladeless handle of his sickle, suspended from his neck, performed in its wearer's hand the function of a quizzing glass.   These shocking evidences of dissipation drew down upon the new comer the sharp rebukes of old Time. His reproofs, however, were "more in sorrow than in anger," and the old gentleman turning to me, assured me that these aberations from the right road were only seldom, and always the unfortunate result of unavoidable circumstances.

"I will show you that young man," said he, "night after night dying his locks gray in the smoky fumes of his lamp, and wasting his pale cheek over his midnight studies to benefit the world. But hark what he has to say for himself."

I turned my head towards the culprit guest, and observed that he was trying to steady himself by leaning upon One and Two O'clock, who to my surprise now began to put on entirely different characters.

"Gentlemen," he at last stammered out, "I ask to be forgiven—I have been in bad company, and have had no Burgundy to drink. But you know it's my nature to be always last—'but better late than never.' Shall I tell you what glorious mortals have been with me to night? Well, they were—they were good fellows—they said I was 'the very witching time of night,' and when I was going, they told me if I could'nt stay I must send my little brother One. Father Chronos, your blessing—gentlemen, my love to you. I drink the hours, all the hours, and nothing but the hours."

Here the crazy spirit observing me, broke through all restraint, and pitching his body in a straight direction towards me, extended both arms for an embrace. I hastily sought to avoid him by getting under the table, but in the attempt I struck my head with a cruel violence against its sharp corner. The blow for a moment stunned me. At last I recovered, and raising my head, found that I was back in church. The gloom of evening was gathering about me; the pulpit and pews were vacant, and the sexton coming up, told me he wanted to close the doors.

ADDRESS OF DR. CYPRESS,

ON TAKING THE ETYMOLOGICAL CHAIR IN THE NEW COLLEGE.

[Published by desire of the class.]

" ETYMOLOGY," says Jeremy Bentham, " is an essential and useful branch of philology. It supposes an acquaintance with the philosophy of the human mind, with the analogies which form and distinguish each language, with the history of mankind, philosophical, religious, and political. It furnishes the readiest and most effectual means to acquire the knowledge of language, and as language is but the dress of our ideas, it holds up a mirror to delineate and reflect the operations of the human mind."

Most authentic art thou, O Jeremy! and whoso readeth with a right spirit, he shall be edified. But all are not true believers. The scepticism and bad taste of this rail road age reject faith, and cry out for demonstration. This is near at hand for the learned caviler; Heaven help the common herd, that cannot comprehend a thing when it is made manifest unto them. We, be it lamented, have got to fight a fight against them. Ay, such is the jealous suspicion of the vulgar world, that in the prosecution of these sublime meditations, we must prepare to combat the prejudices and objections of many a Zoilus, and be solemn as well as earnest, lest they who never studied astrology or magical harmonies, should esteem us to be triflers. Let me remark to these last mentioned, miserable individuals, that, sinful, they are plunged into the same gall of bitterness which drowned the wits of the would-be-wise men, who denied to Columbus a western continent ; that they are obligors upon the same bond of iniquity with the phil-agnosiasts who doubted the circulation of the blood, or the efficacy of vaccination, or who now, impious! shake their profane heads at Captain Symnes and Dædalian Mr. Bennett.

But instead of railing, I should be studious [whispers discretion] of submissive and alluring speech——*ad mulcendos animos*——for engaging the favor of the ignorant, whom I would enlighten. In accordance with this presumption, let me, with deep deference, submit, that the dignity of etymological pursuits is proved by their antiquity, and the character of their patrons.

Herodotus records, that one Samuel Metticus, an ancient king of Egypt, who had a vigorous taste for philosophy, and who would certainly, had he lived in our age, have invented steamboats, and discovered "the" perpetual motion ; being desirous to ascertain what language was the earliest, caused two infants to be taken from their mother's breasts, and confined in a solitary hut, where no human voice might reach them ; very justly and sagaciously determining that if ever they agreed to talk, it would be in the language of nature, and consequently, in that of the first inhabitants of the world. " Ταυτα δ' εποιετο κχι ενετελλετο ο'ψαμματικος," or as it is rendered in Dr. Parr's translation, " these things commanded princely Sam." The babes continued so long mute, that the king began to doubt the wisdom of his theory, when wonderful to be told ! one morning upon the entrance of his servants to feed them with their accustomed meal of goat's milk, the little infants fell upon their knees——Βεκος εφωνεον ορεκοντα τα ς χειρα ς——and, with

uplifted hands, cried out " Bekos." Now had the king understood English, he might readily have perceived that Βεκος is by
apocope Βεκ and by paragoge Βεκκι, or, in our vernacular, *Bekky* ;
and what could " *Bekky*" mean, but a nurse, or servant girl
——a being for whom the unprotected state of the little inno-
cents languished ! And what is consequent, but that there
is a truth in the doctrine of innate ideas, and that one of the
first we entertain is the sense of imbecility ; and that, when
infants, we must be attended by a servant maid, or——by syne-
doche——a *Bekky*, which is a sort of generic term for the whole
tribe ? Or Βεκος indeed, when evolved from juvenile gums,
with the emollient lubricity of an infant lisp, might fall upon
auriculars sufficiently philological, as a well-defined outcry
for *breakfast*——an exclamation extremely natural for hungry
children, and quite common even at the present day. But
both these cogent explications were strangers to Sam. Metticus, whose library had not been furnished with Webster's
Universal, and therefore knew not English undefiled ; and
he finding the oracular word to signify *bread* in some other
language, the question was settled to the infinite detriment
and damage of our mother tongue.

Shakspeare had a very proper idea of the importance of
these pursuits, when he made Hamlet, that courtier, scholar
and soldier, answer to an inquiry of what he studied, " words,
words, words."

The Jewish Rabbins employed themselves in analysing
the words of the Old Testament, well convinced that every
one contained in it a law or a prophecy.

It would be " wasteful and ridiculous excess," to enumerate all the syllabic and literary philosophers, who have spent
their lives in settling the meaning and orthodoxy of words.
The simple proverb, " *verbum sapienti*," will put the dignity

of the profession beyond a doubt. "A word for the wise"
—evidently intending, that it is for wise men alone, to comment on and quarrel about obscure expressions.   We have,
therefore, assumed a weighty responsibility, in putting on the
whole armor of an etymologist, and we must be strong, and
brave, and bold to sustain ourselves in that glorious company
of knights-noscent, who have consecrated themselves to
the overthrow of delusion.   But do not fear for me, my gentle pupil, I have fought for a word before now.   I know the
temper of my weapon, and not without confidence have I
plunged into black blood.

Let us now rush "*in medias res*."   Mark how obscurity
bites the dust, and error gives up the ghost.

The poet very truly and happily sings,

> "The man that hath not music in his *sole*,
> Nor is not moved with concord of sweet sounds,
> Is fit for treasons, stratagems and spoils,"

Now, the vulgar editions have so arranged the last word
in the first line of this triplet, as to make the poet require
every man to keep a music book under his ribs, and that his
soul should be no better than a wind instrument!   Here has
been grievous misconception, and here is our vocation exalted.
The discriminating antiquary and judicious critic, who is
aware of the constant corruption of language, who under-
stands the analogy of words, and is familiar with the manners and customs of nations, will perceive, upon a little reflection, that the poet, in reality, refers to the custom of dancing with musical instruments attached to the feet; having
in his eye, no doubt, the concluding couplet of Herrick's
beautiful little epicedium on the death of Mrs. Malaprop:

> "With rings on her fingers and *bells on her toes*,
> And she shall have music *wherever* she goes."

With this explanation the author's meaning is apparent. Not *Psyche*, nor *alma*, nor the old fashioned English *soul* was in his thought. He is the eulogist of saltation, merely, and superinducent melody. The man, says he,—translated into prose,—who is too Cassius-like to dance, who confesses not the bewilderment and strong compulsion of a tinkling foot, is fit for treason, and all those other things afterwards above mentioned. With what exceeding beauty is the passage invested, by this integration!

Again : It is well settled among Latin scholars, that the word " Lucus," a gloomy grove, derives its name, " *a non lucendo ;*"—that is to say, it is called a bright and cheerful region, because it is black and dark as Erebus. What light is thrown, by this example, upon the obscurity of that beautiful, but much abused line,

"My wound is great because it is so small ?"

Nothing could be more quaintly, yet more naturally conceived.

By the same rationale, my reverend Hellenian professor derived the word *plough* from the Greek verb φλεγω—to burn —because we do not put fiery horses to the aforesaid agricultural chariot.

But instead of multiplying minor instances, to magnify the excellence of our studies, let me call you to the contemplation of one great example, which will afford us all the argument and illustration we can desire. Listen and you shall be edified by the discussion of a much agitated verse of Shakspeare, a compilation of the various readings, and a criticism, modest and conclusive, upon them all. It is no more than justice to that respectable dramatist, that this matter should be settled. It shall be settled now ; and I invoke the shades of Theobald and Dr. Johnson, whom I think I see in the midst of you, to

13*

bear with me to the end, and then pronounce if my success be not complete.

It is well known, that never was bard so favored by posterity, in quantity and variety of commentators and expositors, as he of Stratford. The mass of confusion and obscurity thrown upon his plays, by ignorant editors, and by finical, capricious actors, rendered them, for a long time, of little repute. At last, however, Etymology came to give the deerstealer justice. And when he had lived his little day, the million assumed the prerogative of literary popes, and issued *bulls* for his apotheosis. Then began the worship, and then flourished the contest, who should best understand and most admire. Critic succeeded critic, " buffeting and cuffing each other," as says the erudite-Mr. Seward, each succeeding one accusing his predecessor of stupidity and absurdity. All, however, concurred in this one sentiment—that the author upon whom they commented could have written nothing but sense. Of the immortal bard none dared say, " *aliquando bonus dormitat Homerus.*" Adopting their understood and universally conceded premises, we will join these lovers of darkness rather than of light, and proceed to the contemplation of our text. It may be found in Othello, act fifth, scene second. It is part of the soliloquy of the Moor, after he has entered the bed-chamber, and is commonly read,

" Put out the light, and then put out the light."

This is the reading adhered to by Malone, who refers the first " light" to the candle which the Moor holds in his hand, and the last to Desdemona's life. All this, in his opinion, is spoken in a calm, matter-of-course style. I will first put out the candle, and then I 'll kill my wife.

Warburton thinks, that more emphasis should be laid upon

the latter part of the line, and he accordingly puts a dash after the word " then," leaving it thus—

> " Put out the light, and then—put out the light."

But here a difficulty arises. How shall the last " light" be pointed ? By a period, a mark of interrogation, or of exclamation ? " Put out the light."—" Put out the light !"—or " Put out the light ?" All these lections have their respective advocates ; but as I shall reject them all, I will not at present scan their merits. Let me merely remark that Mr. Hewlett, the celebrated Ethiopian buskin-stretcher, goes the period entirely. He puts a dash after " then," leaving time to Othello to make up his mind about what he will do ; and after being buried in a brown—qr. black—study, and thrumming on his thorax for some fifteen minutes, he suddenly catches at the just born idea, which is almost made visible by his demoniac leap to grasp it—then pulls a suitable quantity of wool out of his head, and with a Kean-flashing eye exclaims, " Put out the light !"

Professor McClearer, of the Dublin university, county Leinster, is quite confident that the last " light" refer's to Desdemona's eyes ; and he therefore proposes to throw light upon the subject, by taking away one " light," and substituting " sight." And, in truth, even Fielding—whose lucubrations, hereupon, are *e profundis*—vehemently swears, that when on his journey in the other world, he heard some literary ghost insist to Shakespeare himself, that the line ought to run,

> " Put out, &c.————————thy eyes."

To me, however, this appears but the turning of light into darkness, so incomprehensible is the insinuation, that even a Turk might imagine a revenge so exquisitely Blackhawkical. Still, it is but fair to admit, that some little color is given to the barbarism, by the assimilated phraseology of Publius Maro, in discoursing of the expelled vision of the one-eyed pastoral giant, who ate up the friends of Ulysses—

"*Monstrum horrendum, informe, ingens, cui lumen ademptum*"—

"The horrible, great monster, whose light was taken away, or put out." But I cannot, nevertheless, admit that the exopthalmation of Polyphemus, which was certainly appropriate, and exceedingly poetical, in its place, can justify the bad taste of making a soldier, and a general, too, put out the two fair eyes of a christian lady.

That learned and ingenious critic, Lampas Lampados, in the one hundred and forty-fifth chapter of his treatise of this line, comes to the conclusion, that the second "light" refers to the same object as the first ; and the latter part of the line is nothing but a natural repetition of the earnest and determined resolution ; Othello meaning, by the word "light" in both clauses, the holy man who married him ; "against whom," says he, " on that accounte he justlie entertaineth a feelinge of revenge and bittternesse, for that he was the architecte of all his miserie." And this dogmatist very cunningly supports his opinion, by an allusion to the torch which Hymen is supposed to hold—a light "ever bright and ever burning" —insisting that the light itself is taken, by metonymy, for the man who holds it. "And this suggestion," he proceeds, " is set arounde and fortified by the contexte."

"If I quench thee, thou ' flaming *minister*,' or thou ill-starred parsonne, which shall presentlie burne, as he might haue sayd. Whence it appeareth, that the succeeding lines, in the vulgate, are but the player's trashe and bombaste. Doe not men commonlie calle a minister, a light, a fire, a light upon the house-tops, a light to kindle and consume the peccant and errant humours of moral morbositie, a lamp, a watch-tower, a pharos, or light-house, to illumine the pathe of his besotted congregation ? Thus then, it seemeth to me : Othello saith, ' Put out the light,' or ' quench the minister ;' evidentlie meaning to drown him in a horse-ponde at some convenient season. Then breakinge off suddenlie, he approacheth the bed-side, when ensueth the final conversation with Desdemona, which endeth with the Moor's passion and her takinge off.''

Sac-Speare, or talking Jim, an eleve of Governor Cass, and secretary of the Columbia-river academy, in a late contribution to the Menomine Quarterly, elaborately reviews the writings of Lampados, and treats this particular subject with much and quite original perspicacity. He attributes great honor to his author, and agrees with him, but in the respect only that he considers that the last " light" refers to the ceremonial of the nuptials. " We give light credence," says he, " to the presumption that our seraphic ancestor ever wrote such words, meaning simply and tamely thereby to repeat the same idea. The swan does not so˙sing. The governor of all Cyprus did not so think. Mystery, not simplicity, is the fountain of the sublime. The bard has here availed himself of that excellent provision of his king's English, which compels a single word to stand godfather for many ideas. We doubt not that he forsaw the anxious interest and distress of posterity to know the truth of the matter, and that this line gave him more satisfaction than any he ever wrote." Under the arrangement of this writer, the interpretation of the perplexity would be, " put out," or " get rid of the light of Hymen's torch, or the old friar, and then I can get rid of the marriage itself—*i. e.* remove all evidence, and who shall say that I am married to her ?" To illustrate and enforce this new application of " light," the reviewer refers to a similar figure in Ovid's Metamorphoses,* where the Sulmonian speaks of Diana's refusal of Apollo's hand ;

"Ille velut crimen *tædas* exosa *jugales*."

Here is certainly a singular coincidence of thought, and the secretary may be correct ; at all events, he makes a most respectable show of argument.†

But what says the Italian monk, Claraluce, a contemporary of Lampados? He strikes out the whole of the soliloquy after the sixth line, " yet she must die," &c., and is positive that "put out the light" is only a direction to the stage-manager, and that it was originally inserted in the margin. And this, for the reason that a sudden darkness ought to come over the stage, when any terrible deed is about being enacted by such a murderous villain as Othello. And he cites, characteristically enough, the authority of Job xviii. 5, " Yea, the light of the wicked shall be put out ; the spark of his fire shall not burn."

Another writer, with equal boldness, agrees to the nullification of the concluding part of the soliloquy ; but thinks that "put out," &c., was part of an old snatch which Othello be-

---

* Book 1, line 484.

† The descent of Sac-speare from the family of the poet of Stratford, is now too well established to admit of a doubt. The editor of the National Gazette has satisfactorily shown, in his " Parakalummata Hamerikana,"t hat Shakspeare's youngerb rother,—who was enamored of the same fair eyes, which drew from Will his sweetest sonnet,—sick with disappointment, and disgusted with the world, accompanied a band of Moravian missionaries on their pious pilgrimage to Kamschatka. Thence travelling on foot, to the northeasternmost point of Asia, he crossed Behring's straits in an Indian canoe, and followed the lakes southward, until he fell in with a hunting party of the St. Regis Indians. Being lean, meagre and apostrophical in his appearance, they readily adopted him as their prophet ; and his half-blood descendants enjoyed that dignity for many years. The subject of the present note was taken prisoner in one of the border skirmishes during the late war, and his blood and bearing soon found for him a Mæcenas.—*Walsh Par. Ham. p.* 384.

gan to sing, to keep his spirits up, and induce a feeling of composure and indifference, during the commission of his horrid crime ; just as a soldier drinks brandy and gunpowder, upon the eve of his engagement in battle. And he conjures up, from the purgatory of deceased and forgotten ballads, this verse, the last remnant of a precious combination of sentiment and simplicity :

> " Then out spoke Will, that cunning wighte,
>   Looking all tenderlie,
>   Economie is a virtue, Sal,
>   We do not need to see ;
> For if lovers can say all they would i'th' darke,
> It were sinful to waste a whole candle to sparke,
>   And soe put out the lighte.
>   Put out, &c.
>   Put out, &c.
> Come let's put out the lighte."

It must be confessed, that all these readings are enforced by such cogent argument, that it is difficult to choose between them ; for any one of them, separately considered, appears incontrovertible. But after a thorough investigation of the subject, I am convinced that none of them have half so good a claim to confidence, as a reading of my own, which I shall presently propound. First, it is my duty, as a faithful reviewer, to enumerate some inferior readings, which, although not commanding much respect, are entitled to a recapitulation.

> " Put out, &c.—and then pull out my wife."
> " Put out—and then pull out my knife."
> " Put out—and then—but if you bite."
> " Put out—and then to my delight."
> " Put out this light, and then put out that light."

This is the reading of Mr. Claudius Lucerne, an eminent literary tallow chandler, who thinks Othello must have had six-to-the-pound in each hand.

> " Put out the light, and then pull down the wall."

This, as one might readily suppose, is the proposed version of a matter-of-fact man, like Cobbett. He points, with all the air of triumph of a discoverer of the truth, to Cynthio's novels, whence the plot of the play is taken; and where the story runs, that the Moor killed his spouse, by pulling down upon her bed, a decayed part of the wall, hoping, the craven! that the coroner's jury would bring in a verdict of " Death by the prolapsion of lath and plaster."

> "Butter my eyes, but I'll put out the light."

Jam satis. Since there are so many plausible versions, I am verecund of the pronunciation of a positive judgment in the matter. But, as no man should hide the light of his reason under a bushel, but bring it, even if a farthing candle, to the illumination, I will break through the thick array of my modesty, and unfold the only true, genuine and original reading, such as Shakspeare wrote it, and such as Etymos Logos revealed it to me.

> "Put out the light, and then—put! into bed."

I approve this arrangement, firstly, because it is most consonant with nature. This is sometimes a good rule to go by, in the settlement of obscure and disputed passages, when the resolution so made is palpable. [I followed it lately, in one instance, myself, in translating Æsculapius, for the college in Barclay street.] And what can be more natural and reasonable, in a man worn out with the toils of the day, than to go to his bed chamber, put out his candle, and repose himself in the arms of nature's sweet restorer? I never can admit that Shakspeare intended to make the Moor guilty of so bloodthirsty a design, as the vulgate imputes to him; because it would have been unnatural, and at war with the all-prevailing and irresistible organ of go-to-bediviness.

Secondly. In answer to the objection that this reading is inconsistent with the spirit of the play, and the preconceived intentions of Othello, it is sufficient to remark, that such cavils are opposed to the spirit of free inquiry, and that it is the beauty of this particular line, and not the probability or consistency of the whole plot, that we are considering; and that this rule has been the constant rudder of judgment of all commentators, from the time whereof the memory of man runneth not to the contrary.

Thirdly and lastly. By a very simple course of explanation, it may be shown that the corrupted reading in common acceptation, is but a finical version of what Shakspeare wrote. The alteration of the original text was made by the players for the sake of euphony, and the swell of figurative language; and it consists in nothing more than the substitution of " out the light" for " into bed." The difficulty is then removed, the problem is resolved. " Into bed" means nothing more or less than " out," or " out of the light ;" for what is is plainer than that when a man gets into bed, and covers his head over, he is in the dark? Or " out the light" may be used by a sort of figure of anticipation, for " into bed," since it was a well known custom among the people in Cyprus— a custom from which William the Conqueror took his idea of the curfew regulation—to extinguish their candles before the submitting themselves to Morphean influences. Again ; the prepositions " out" and " into" were promiscuously used for each other, by all the respectable writers of the Elizabethan age. Thus, Cyprian, the younger, in describing the martyrdom and sufferings of St. Trollopea, with beautiful pathos utters those now almost household words, " out of the frying-pan into the fire." And an acquaintance with etymology will discover that they are frequently interchanged, to avoid tauto-

Vol. II.—14

logy. The word " bed " may perhaps be called " the light,"
from the lightness of the feathers of which it is composed.
The only difficulty, then remaining undisposed of, is that
which arises from the construction of the word " put." This
I take to be simply, a particle, which here signifies ease,
self-complacency, good nature, rub-your-hands-togetherive-
ness,—as Gall and Spurzheim call it, affability and amative-
ness ; and I account it to be a word of exceeding pith, point
and expression, exclusive and authentic, and most happily
introduced on this occasion. " Is this fancy, or is it fact ?"
Is it not clear as light itself ?

> " How far a little candle sheds its light !
> So shine true readings through a misty world."

What, then, remains for me, but to call for your special
plaudits, and remove the light of my countenance ? Nothing,
but a few peroratorical comments by way of reflection on
the subject.

     *   *   *   *   *   *

NEWSPAPERS.

" *Quid novi ?*"—" *What's the news ?*"—Demosthenes lectured his acres-spread congregation, once for asking this
question, when Philip of Macedon was on their boundary
line, without opposition, and his countrymen were without
means of defence. "Ἡ βόλεσθε," said he, " εἰπέ μοι, περιϊόντες αὐτῶν
πυνθάνεσθαι κατὰ τὴν ἀγορὰν, λέγεταί τι καινόν ?"

Is there no Demosthenes in Columbia ? Are the orators
voiceless ?—or corrupt all ? Heartless ! Is it possible that

we can content ourselves by running about and asking " what is the news?" are we readers only, and not doers? Do we lie in bed and comfortably read, in print, how splendidly our brother fell, cut with a Floridian tomahawk? Do we prefer *" to read"* the account of the atrocities perpetrated by her Majesty's Most particular Lieutenant Governor of ALL the Canadas on the suffering chickens of Bill Jones' farm? Do we choose to sleep and dream, upon the authority of the printer-devil-children of Dr. Faustus, of the invasion of the Spaniard and the Camanche at the South-west—of the stealthy insinuation of the Russ at Columbia River,—or the skulking policy of " negotiation" of our own selves with regard to the boundary line of Maine !——

" Yes. Yes. Yes."——

" Who the devil are you! Jack, my dear boy, I'm glad to see you. You came in quiet, then, and looked over my shoulder—ha?"

" Those are my precise sentiments."

" The"——

" I say that we, the people of the United States of America, are a set of cowards and sneaks."

" Moderate, Jack, moderate."

" I insist that there is not a spark of soul or pluck left in the republic. People have got quicksilver running through their veins instead of blood. I swear——"

" Don't swear, Jack. What do you lay it to?"

" Lay it to? I lay the whole at the door of the newspapers."

" Why so, my dear fellow, why so?"

" Now," said Jack, " I shall, like enough, make some rough and harsh remarks, which, knowing as I do your attachment to the Press—and the Press-gang is a big power, and always stamps the man killing the lion—reasons in the money drawer ;——"

" Jack, none of your gammon. Take your finger off your nose——"

" ——I say, then, I mean there is not a paper in this country whose columns may not be bought. They belong to, are supported by, and paid for by PARTIES. They are merely hired agents, like the Brummagem 'travellers' dressed up in clean shirts, and dispatched abroad for customers *for* particular houses, all of them taking pains to avoid the general good. They would sacrifice their country to benefit their own selfish ambition. Each pretends that he is the man, and that wisdom will die with his party."

" But, Jack, what parties ? You surely don't include the religious papers. Think of the ' Deserver.' "

" Deserver ! Why, do you suppose I am capable of believing that the Editor of that ably conducted Presbyterian oracle would record the dying faith and pious decadence from earth, and ascent to Heaven of a Catholic Priest ?"

" But then take the ' Verity Teller,' Jack. What objections, if you are a subject of the Pope, have you to that ?"

" None ; none, my friend, but upon the score of its being a party paper. The Deserver says that their—Deserving—party will go to Heaven. The Verity Teller tells them that they lie, and that they'll go to Hell. The different members of the crafts meet in the day time, and buy and sell, and cheat each other, and one goes home at night and prays for the crushation of Antichrist, and the other goes to an *earthly* 'Father,' and ' confesses' that he hath had dealings with an Heretic. Both having absolved themselves, by praying God's curses on each other, they meet again next day, and trade and sin until the hour of prayer and confession."

" Jack, are you sincere in this ?"

" Sincere ? Look at their files. Nothing but fire, shot, bang, blast, attack, storm, cut, slash, and the devil. Hughes and Breckenridge, Christian and Appollyon all over. But this isn't to the point. What I meant to say was, that with all their pious zeal, I can buy both those papers. I can make the ' Deserver' Catholic, and the ' Verity Teller' Presbyterian to-morrow."

" You're a fool."

" That's what was said to Columbus and Ben Franklin. Havn't you lived long enough in this world to learn that people now-a-days profess principles for money's sake ? Are the editors of either of those papers apostles, living on their own hooks———"

" Jack, you're blasphemous."

" God forbid ! I meant nothing about those glorious Heaven-appointed, being fishermen——who worked for love merely, ——but intended merely to ask *does anybody preach, teach, write, or speak in these modern of times without being paid for the service ?* Is not talent a thing to be bought, and wisdom a commodity in the market ? Is it public good that induces a poor scholar to set up a paper ?——to stake his all upon a fount of types ? Or is it not the hope of gain, or at least a livelihood ? What writer throws the bread of his own baking upon the waters of the ocean, trusting, on a false credit hope, that it will come back to him buttered, with a fish fast hold of it ?"

" Stop ; stop ; you impetuous cynic. I say yes ; yes ; yes. It *is* public good that has made many ' a poor scholar' write, and many a benevolent man-angel speak. Think of the quaker preachers ! They get no pay."

14*

"None but world applause. Dr. Cox thinks their drafts on heaven will all be dishonored."

"Jack, you are the most incorrigible——Change the subject—change the subject—some other line of news—stages."

"Be it so."

"What do you think of the magazines?"

"Most decidedly all for party and profit. Mere meadow-hens, looking out for their families. Picking up is their vocation. How gloriously they can persuade an ambitious graduate that it will be to his eternal happiness to be in their mouth, like a soft shelled crab!"

"But, Jack, they must live."

"Truly so. But not honorably, nor morally at other men's expenses. Do they ever hand the plate in the church, to the pews where the *poor communicants sit?*"

"But the magazine publishers pay their correspondents, don't they?——I don't mean out of mere charity."

"When a contributor gets his name '*up*' they do. Let a writer get *established* and he can write any manner of non-sense, and the discriminating public will cry 'beautiful!' and the proprietors of the magazine will look the respectfully amiable, and contribute back. But let a man be unknown, no matter how good his article, and he has the solitary satis-faction of seeing himself *in print.*"

"Well, they are honest—impartial, and free from 'Party,' are they not?"

"Are you so innocent as to ask that question? Why, one is mercantile, another law, another mechanical, another philo-sophical, another moral, another military, another political, another religious, another anti-masonic, another abolition, ano-ther——"

" Hold up, Jack. Do you mean to say that these all represent different parties ?"

" Most distinctly. They all belong to a particular interest. An independent article in any one of them, acknowledging the hope of salvation of another, would effectually damn the bold admitter. The patrons would send in an immediate discontinuance. Why, our friend Harry—who writes, you know, for several of them,—has to select his subject, accommodate his sentiments, study his style, and pick his words. At seven P. M. he will write a sermon for 'the Watchman on the Wall,'—at nine 'a few remarks on snakes' for the 'Philosophical Observer,'—at ten 'the last moments of Jane Shore' for the 'Ladies' Maga,'—at eleven 'Abolition on the Railroad of Success" for ' Garrison's Glory,' and then go to bed like a good carpenter after his day's work."

" But, dear Jack, how does this hurt the country ? How can you say that our liberties or virtue are endangered, or the happiness of the republican family prejudiced by the conflicts of opinion or taste ? Ought we not to have parties to balance the——"

" Now, that is as silly a proposition as the nursery ballad of

> 'Jack Sprat could eat no fat,
> His wife could eat no lean ;
> And so it was, betwixt them both
> They licked the platter clean.'

Do you seriously believe that it is necessary to have ' parties' in the country to save our glorious Constitution ? And do they not keep the country in a constant ferment, setting son against father, and neighbor against neighbor ?——"

" Jack, there must be parties. Eternal watchfulness——"

" Gammon, gammon ! You put me in mind of the daily press."

" Well, what of that ?"

" That's what I began on ;—the vilest, truckling, sycophantic, hypocritical, money-begging, proud-swaggering, empty-headed, encyclopedia-thieves——"

" ——Some exceptions, Jack ?"

" Few, few. They all boast of their exclusive virtue, and damn their neighbors."

" The ' Dispatch and Asker' is a good paper ?"

" Meat-axe all over. When I take it up I consider myself entering a butcher's knife-shop. Cut, cut, strike, cut, for our party, is the cry of the ' leader.' There is not an honest man in the world but belongs to us. ' Exterminate the rascals, and then we'll have a new fight among ourselves,' is all the talk, and all the patriotism."

" What have you to say against the quiet ' Columbian ?' "

" Quiet ? quiet! Yes, how quietly it honored the dead wife of General Jackson, for party's sake. A woman—dead !"

" I won't say a word to you on that head, Jack. I've no doubt it's sorry for it. Party spirit——"

" Yes, that's the very thing I am telling you of. It was the same print that came out with a recommendation to every man to reject his son, every mother to turn her daughter out of doors, every sweet girl to dismiss her lover, every brother to strike his brother, every friend to deny his friend, who did not belong to *his* or her party."

" That's rather on the horrid, Jack. What have you got against the ' Evening Rail ?' "

" Party all over. Party, ' us,' ' we' and public printing. There is powerful writing there, and some truth, but it is often askew. The everlasting looking out for ' the greatest good of the greatest number,' leads the editor too much to

magnify Fly Market loafers into the conservators of the country, and minify decent men into bloodsuckers. The best of
the instructive 'leaders' are full of cool, deliberate, party
heat. They are paid for."

"Well, you are a queer one. Whom will you except?
What do you say to the 'Animal Magnetism Advertiser?'"

"No let up. The bitterest partisan—methodistical and
solemn its partizanship ; It would take the Canadas for itself,
by artifice, but write against the true soldiers of the Republic
entering them by bravery."   •

"What against the 'Quicksent?'"

"A mere made thing, baked out of the ashes of two or
three dead prints. It knows barely enough to help to distract
the public comfort by joining in the chorus of 'Ruin,' which
the Dispatch leads the air to."

"Journal of Merchandize?"

"There's an exception. I believe that paper is pure. It
is good, at all events, and it tells the story on both sides. If
you have acid in one column, you have soda in the next.
You may mix up Amos Kendall and Daniel Webster, and
have a right good drink."

"What do you think of the penny papers?"

"Some are strong ; almost all good ; but *their* excellence
arise from their freedom from party thrall. Where they *do
owe* allegiance, they are slaves, and can talk no freer language than an English clodhopper. But I am interrupting
you. I only called in to say how d'ye do. What the deuce
was you going to write when I came in?"

"I can't say, Jack, I forget. You put me out. It was
something about newspapers—I was going to praise them,
but you have put a twist into my pen, and belied the craft.

I shall have to do the thing over.   The liberty of the press, the glorious freedom of thought, the———"

"I see the fit is on you yet.   Good bye."

"Good bye, Jack.   But don't be in a hurry.   Hold on half a minute.   What do you think of 'the Moon?'"

"It's like all moons—it has its changes.   It has its phases.   It sometimes runs high, and sometimes runs low.   It professes great morality, talks windy solemnity in its editorials, as though it was learned and serious upon every subject —Newton to-day, Beethoven yesterday, Napoleon to-morrow, Channing next day, Recorder Riker the day following.   Successive sermons stamp its editorial columns.   But look at its advertising part—can you find anything more filthy than the constant notices about 'no mercury'—'French specific'—'no quackery'—'to the ladies,' and so on?   I cannot speak the infamy of the accumulated titles.   'Rapes,' 'robberies,' 'murders,' 'coroner's inquests,' and all sorts of police reports, of the most disgusting detail."

"You are pretty much of my sentiments."

"I see that you and I agree that all papers belong to some clique or party.   Now, I say that the Moon is a party paper.   It belongs to the no-party-party, and to that class of people who need secret quack medicines, and lose dogs and cows, and who like advertisements of drinking-shops, and can tolerate lectures on temperance.   But it will never hurt the country as the partisan warriors do, and there is really much talent thrown away upon its leaders.   But its columns, instead of teaching American boys the pride of National Honor, more effectually call their young eyes to the 'Quid novi' of the Police office and the Five Points."

"Why, Jack, you beat all men I ever heard talk.   Pray how does 'the Herald' stand in your estimation?"

" I don't know the coin, my friend. But to return to general observations. It is safer than to particularize. The newspaper press throughout the whole Union is by its own confession, and by its mutual proofs against each other, the mere organ of ambition, selfishness, and humbug. They usurp, it is true, the places of the ancient orators, and dictate morals and patriotism to the country. But you do not hear Cicero ;— you recognise not the pure flame of Grecian boldness, that threw itself into the mob, and storm-like, dashed out the fire of plebeian madness. The difference between our ditors eand ancient orators is something like that between garden fireworks and Heaven's lightning. Would any of the old-times voice-strikers for liberty have ended his speech with a notice that ' Jacobus Corvus *had* a farm for sale at 12 M. at the capitol—terms easy ?'—wouldn't he have fallen at the feet of Pompey's statue ? or been torn to pieces ? Now look at the successors of the orators ! Read their affectation first, and then look at their proof. " We call the particular attention of our readers to the sale of the splendid building lots at Frog-pond, advertised to be sold this day at 12 M., by Blinker and Book, auctioneers." For the same hour you see—" We must not forego the opportunity to remind our friends ! that the sale of Colonel Bankem's delightfully situated building lots on Prospect Hill comes off to-day at 12 M." Next—" It is expected that Mr. Preston will address his fellow citizens at 12 M. this day, from the steps of the Astor House. No true friend of the country should be absent. Citizens who have got them, are requested to appear in white pantaloons, on horseback." Next—" Our readers will bear in mind that the sale of all the imported blood stock of Creature Comfort, Esq., is to take place to-day at 12 M., at the Exchange. The horses will make a fine stud. No true lover of his country should be absent." Then——" Remember! 12 is the time Mr. Ascent starts his balloon from Castle Garden. That invaluable citizen, Mr. Marsh, the proprietor, has provided extensive accommodations, and no friend of industrious enterprise should be wanting, for any consideration. Let no one be absent."

"This is a specimen of editorials. Call you it honest ?—— Independent ? Free from party falsehoods and gull-traps ? Are they not all paid for ? Who cracked up the miserable speculations in town lots and wilderness tracts, in the wretched speculation times, but the newspaper editors ? How many a trusting fool was gulled by the editorial lie of ' *We take pleasure to call the attention of our readers,*' &c. ? Which daily theatre puff shall we now-a-days, out of the six or eight, believe ?"

"Jack ! Jack ! you'll get into the papers yourself. They'll put you in for high treason !"

"Damn 'em, let 'em do it, and I'll give them more truth. They're ruining the country. The police ought to stop them. The Chancellor ought to issue an injunction against them. They all go against Vice, but they teach its existence, so that they may have a chance to abuse it, and clarion their own health, while they pamper, or poison, or create subjects for new articles. There is such a thing in criminal law as ' *crimen non nominandum ;*'——but these collectors of rottenness, paste, as it were, the name upon their forehead, and stand in the street for curious, innocent purchasers—perhaps virgins ! If things are not sufficiently ' rank and gross in nature,' they or their reporter—horrid office ! Rag-picker ! Street-sweeper ! Kennel-cleaner !——must pepper more filth of prurient imagination into it——"

"Hallo ! Hallo ! Jack !"

" Where are the fathers of the city who tolerate such *news*. papers ?—Here, take up a number of one of them by chance ; it is the number for August, 13th, 1840. First is a puff of themselves, and their success. Next a part encyclopedia and part magazine copied sermon set up as ' original matter,' on the much vexed question whether a countryman ought to be allowed to charge more than sixpence a-piece for his chickens now, in consideration of the state of the currency. Then a sprinkling of more gammon. Then—the cream of the paper—' Fatal accident'—' State prison'—' Shall not be surprised if we before long hear of some act of desperation' —*alias*, kill your sentinels, and come to the city—then ' Inquest'—on a—fallen woman—' Indians'—' Shocking sui-cide'——"

" Jack, don't go too far. "

" My friend I've not gone far enough. If you want evi-dence of the licentiousness and degradation of the press, look at the police reports in that same paper—' Stealing a shawl —a female'—'Stealing dresses—Maria Stone'—' Stealing money and a watch—some person.' But look at the two fol-lowing, entitled ' Disorderly house,' and ' Scenes in Anthony street !'—Great God ! are we not bad enough by nature, but that we need the devil to teach us through the printing-press how to sin, where to sin, and how many others sin ?"

" Well, what would you have ? What the dickens do you want ? Would you go back to old John Lang's time, who wouldn't let more than half a little finger of editorial go into the Gazette, because it did'nt look like business ?"

" I would. A newspaper is not a place to inculcate gene-ral literature and morals, or to lay down the laws, or herald vice. We have books enough, holding the fountain where we can bend and drink for ourselves wisdom and virtue.

Vol. II.—15

Neither is it a proper grammar of politics.   When it becomes a debator, it is an essayist, bought to write up an opinion, instead of a *news*paper.   Old Lang was right.   In place of reading the bought opinions of party hirelings, who would write on the other side for sixpence more to-morrow, let men go home and study the Constitution, and the early history and splendid debates of their old Congresses and Conventions. From them they can imbibe an honest and fervent draught of the freest spirit of freedom, the holiest mounting-foam of liberty, truth untrammelled, glory———"

" *In excelsis*, Jack, keep down lower, or I shall lose sight of you.   You mean to say a man may mis-spend his time in reading newspapers ?"

" I do.   If he reads them all, and pays attention to one-tenth of the saints' days, he'll have no time for the duties of personal life, contract wrong ideas, hurt his health, and crack his brains.   A constant reader of newspapers, instead of wholesome authority, that speaks without party influence, is like an idiot boy who would plunge into a green mant-ling cow-pool, in preference to bathing in the ocean."

" Jack, you're right.   I'll put your sentiments down.   I don't wonder that Cooper is compelled to sue them."

" Nor I.   Farewell once more."

" Good bye."

CATACOUSTICS.

"The sensation which we perceive through the organ of hearing is called sound, such as the sound of a human voice, the sound of a bell, &c. The science which treats of sound in general is called "Acoustics,"—from the Greek word for hearing,—or phonics,—from the Greek word which means voice, or sound.—And most of the other terms which are used in treating of sound, are derived from the above-mentioned words; such as Diacoustics, CATACOUSTICS, &c."

THAT is the philosophy with which Cavello commences his Chapter IX., Part II., entitled—"of Sound, or of Acoustics."

I have been led by reflection upon an intercepted letter, lately embodied in the "Spirit," written by some foreign trollop, touching "The cries of New York," to look a little further into the matter than that shrewd but doubtful specimen of English ladyship had means or ability to snoop. I am glad I have done so, for I have found at least one "American peculiarity" that must be defended from foreign abuse. Cœrlærs Hook, the Five Points, and all those interesting situations in the suburbs, which have been planted with innocent-looking village churches,—all spire and no body,—put up on ragged sticks on barren fields marked out with a sign post, and glorified with the titles of Avenues "A," "B," "C," and "Promise Place," and "After date Square," and "Cashier Row," and "Texas Stroll," and such like;—gemmed with a grogshop, and occasionally honored with a post-office!—Post-Master save the remark!—by some "enterprising" speculator upon the capital of his glib and queer tongue;—and all the plausible "enterprise" of us Yankees to take in friends and fools with solemn assurances of the silver rivulets that are always *going to begin* to run from Penobscot to Lake Ponchartrain ; and all the other tricks and cheateries of the " Enterprise" part of my people, and all the vulgar vices which foreign debasement has brought here ;—these I give and yield in tribute to any trollop who will aspire to criticism, and create for herself a character, by abusing them. These things I surrender. Let deformity illustrate vice. Let vulgarity vomit out the proof of its associations.

But no trollop must abuse the Cats of my native city, either by direct libel or by sarcastic inuendo. The tiger spirit possesses me on this subject, and I scream for cats.

I am for *cat-acoustics*, only.—I have heard of cock-crowing. I have read about the early lark at matin dawn, striking his head against the top of the cage, and of the robin's silver whistle, playing upon wires, and the wren's shrill joyfulness, uplifted from some straggling smoke-dried poplar, and of many other of the varieties of the creaking, piercing, fifery performances of our most cherished city of *Neo Eboracensis*. I have heard a band of music. I went to a *Roar*-atorio,—or Oratorio as they call it,—once, at the Tabernacle. I have heard a woman sing " *Oft in the stilly night*." My next-door neighbor is a Frenchman who has an educated parrot that talks like a judge, who decides by instinct before he hears the argument, and prates and anticipates, and cries his own praises incessantly, " *Pretty Poll ! Pretty Poll !*" in constant and earnest reiteration, interrupted only when he stops to drink—for he is a marvelous member of the temperance society. I have been to a Methodist Camp Meeting. I have been " high," and have sung myself. Whether I *heard* myself, " *de hoc non*." Probably more " *Hoc*" than " non." Over the way, and opposite to me, two little infants are learning " *Isle of beauty, fare the well*," from a spinster teacher ; who, when she gets through her instructive department, goes

into the amusing,—like farce after tragedy,—and screams
" *una voce poco*," in such a way, that your enraptured judgment cries out " *fa !*" before she has poked her " *voce*" fully
into you.   In fact, I have the advantage of great musical experience, even from the booming thunder of a cannon, down
to the maiden squeal of a mouse.   I am a musician.   I affect
not Hayden.   I love not Handel.   They have sublimity, but
no dramatic action in their stately glories.   They march in
column of attack.   Where they strike, they do terrible execution, but they preserve too close a column.

To keep up the military phraseology, they don't *display*
and *turn their enemy's flanks*.   They break down the walls of
your ears, and enter conquerors, but don't cut you up and smash
you.   They achieve a solemn victory, and stop.   Then again,
Bishop, and all that class of Missnancyists are whining babies.
They are competent to set Barbauld's poems, or Tom Moore
Little's Hymns, down into some select public-garden minstrelsy, but they will never grow up into the maturity of musicians.   Other people I have heard, and whose music I know,
and upon whom I set a proper value ; but of all the quadru-
pedal, feathery, or two-footed creation, man or inhuman, woman or fallen ———, next after paying a proper reverence to
the living action of Von Weber's engravings, stamped by the
moonlight from the reflection of the trees and rough ravines of
the Hartz mountains, by his own Daguerreotype, I go for the

Mew-sic
of
Felis

1 am   for
Cat-acoustics.

Here is my gauntlet.   Take it up who dare.   Answer my
cat-echism.

15*

Music is a running thrill that rushes over you with a sensation of almost choaking deliciousness ; like a sudden ocean-wave on a smooth gravelly beach ; isn't it ? Its changes are like the smiles and frowns of a good girl—twenty-five years old ;—or the quick alternations of the politics of the spirits of the air, who, one moment, vote for Cloud, and next, Lightning, and next, Rain, and then, Blue Sky ; ar'n't they ? Music is change, race, flight, fight, mixed love and anger, the tear of sentiment, the gush of passionate outbreak, and several other things ; is'nt it ? Is there any music in " dum, dum, dum, dum, dum, dum ?" Apollo forbid ! Such a performance would be worse than a silent Quaker meeting, or a Scotch bagpipe. But put " *d*' " on the top of the house, where he can have *the air*, and " *u*"—not *you*, my dear—in the front bed-chamber in the second story, and " *m*" in the cellar, and then let the representatives of sound run up and down. " M" will bring with him " blasts from Hell," and " D" drop into the composition, " airs from Heaven," while " U" will do the earthly part of the business, and the appoggiature ladder will multiply its rungs, and be peopled with strange but sweet voices borne to you upon the velocipede above referred to, aud so you'll go to glory. Now what musical instrument made of tongue, teeth, thorax, or wire and ivory, can boast a scale of notes, from the profound of mad rage to the exhausted argute of pathos equal to the shrill delight of the feline gamut ? I drink as a garden drinks dew, the native melodies of a cat. A well-voiced Tom-cat is your true musician of nature. He is Diana's commissioned serenader. History books say that " the wild or mountain-cat is borne in coats-of-arms as the emblem of liberty, vigilence, and forecast." Our city cat has all these honors with the additon of a classical education, cultivated taste, and knowledge of the world. Your peasantry mountain-ridger does very well in the way of his vocation. He screams out fourth fiddle with very good effect. But it takes one of our cultivated urban Toms to fife, fiddle, bassoon, and hurdy-gurdy all together.

The Romans gave their domestic tigers three names; to wit, Felis, Catus, and Catulus. These were probably, different tribes, using different styles of melody. "Felis" was the pre*furred* name, however, and lapped the most plentiful milk of favor. A good mouser was called "Muricida." But to give the *cat*alogue of names might put me in the same *cat*egory with a prosing peasant. That *cat*astrophe I beg leave to avoid, and so go on with my story. Permit me that *felis*ity.

Some people like the voice of a dog. Not I.

The dog bays the moon, and howls out sickness, thirst, and madness, but puss pours out wild and melancholy love-notes in tender, healthful adagio and maestoso. Does he succeed in calling his ladye-love to the old trysting-place so many a night hallowed by fierce and gentle dalliance ;—what soul-piercing epithalamics fill with poetic fury the ear of the sentimental watchman, snoozing hard by! How many a feverish tongue in the chosen happy neigborhood swears out in rapture at the paradisical concert. The Garcia never sung as a cat can sing.

Blessed air! Cavallo says it is "the vehicle of sound." So it is. And what hero can better stride that velocipede than the voice of a cat?

The mariner's welcome of the word "*Catspaw*," comes upon the cloudy cry of distant land-cats, and his sail and soul vibrate together with the greatful impulse of the breeze. He runs to his "*cat-heads*," and heaves up his anchor, and *claws* off to the deep rumbling ocean. It is a singular fact that the word "cat" is as necessary a term of description in music, as any particle is to a particular class of words in prose orthography. This is a well-deserved tribute to the musical genius of that interesting animal. "Cat" in acoustics is what "pro," "con," "ad" &c., are in grammar. The music of the rushing torrent of waters at Niagara cannot be described but as a *cat*-aract. The Paganinies of the world draw their bows upon *cat*gut. Poets sleep upon *cat*tails to get inspiration. If three musicians go home drunk of a moonlight night, they are sure to entertain the town with a cat-ch.

The *courier-avant* critics of the opera, who decide for the people beforehand, join the orchestra with *cat*calls. The printer's devils and general loafers *cat*erwaul. Shakspeare's "Twelfth Night" was acted in that way on Mrs. Wood's last night at the Park, when old Hays came in and cried out, like a true police-officer, in the language of Maria—

"What a *cat*erwauling do you keep here ? If my lady—the Mayor—have not called up her steward, Malvolio,—the captain of the watch,—and bid him turn you out of doors, never trust me."

*Cat*skill mountain is full of the lowing of *cat*tle. The penitentiary *cat*acombs are tragic with the notes of despair. Every ship is vocal with the cat-o'-nine-tails. "Kit" is a small fiddle. Every body can sing that pathetic old English ballad entitled "Dido and Æneas," the burden of which is "*Kitty kit* dink-a-Dido." I could go on, but the illustrations I have given are sufficient for my *purr*pose.

Catacoustics is defined to be the echo or air-copied reflection of the offspring of the sonorous body which utters some new-born melody. How truly apposite is the name when applied to our city cats ! How plentiful are all the needful instruments of reproduction ! Let some battle-worn grimalkin pour out a solitary ditty upon your fence at midnight, and the adjacent walls of the block will catch up the glorious essence of sound, and fling it back and about like the orgies of the most classical wizards. You will dream of Der Freyschutz, and think you hear a spirit. But if you want to be lapped in Elysium, listen to a Cat Concert. To get one up, only tell your cook to leave the dinner remnants on the grass plot, instead of handing them, according to law, to the swill-man. Let it be done on some moonlight night, so that there will be a chance for help to the effect, from the soaring stretch of some late-watching she-eagle—every block furnishes a proper quota—who sits by her window, pounding her piano—no ; forte—and goes E in the sixty-sixth ledger line, sostenato, for a quarter of an hour without breathing. That helps the harmony powerfully. If you can get a man with a hand organ to grind at your front door while the performance is going on, and an amateur of "foreign airs" to saw his guitar and voice to the "native graces" over the way, at the same time, your appointments will be complete—you are happy—very happy.

Such are the *New* York festivals. Is it needful to describe them ? Why do I ask ? Who can describe the effect produced by the chorus of sixty cats, aided by all the musical talent of the ward !

Reader thou hast been at such a concert. Thou hast not ? Hence then, thou knowest naught. First, however, give me a thousand dollars for teaching thee a new pleasure. Pay me the moneys, invite your cats, and call me a good musical *cat*erer.

P. S. If you can throw in a small boy who sings Methodist Hymn tunes *dolorotissima voce*, like the howl of a mad dog, it will put into your conglomerate work, the idea of Death's head on a tombstone. Put alongside of him a young gentleman, who squeals with his sweetheart, harmonious " why-e-a, why-e-a—whew, e, a, a, a, a,   a,   ah !

                            a,   ah ! ah !

                                a,   a,

                                    a,

                                  ah ! ah !

                                      a, ah !

                                    aha !

and the cats will be encouraged by the competition. Cry " Fire !" and " Watch" yourself. Pay the money before specified to the " Spirit," for I have a notion that he's short of funds to feed his *cattle*-laborers, and such. This is the end of the *cata*logue. Now, dearest *Kate*, I am free, but—for—thee.

THE HON. MISS SAUSSAGE'S MAR-RIAGE.

[Reported expressly *Not* for " *The* WEDDING *Observer*," but for " THE SPIRIT OF THE TIMES.]

THE ceremony of the Hon. MISS SAUSSAGE's marriage took place on the 10th instant at the chapel of St. Imitante. This distinguished lady—whose descent and character are so familiar to the whole Christian Marketing world,—so familiarly known as a distinguished representative of the Porkine race of nobility, who take their heraldic devices from the record kept of the *ordines* who went into Noah's ark, and who are so remarkable for the successful warfare which they have kept up with the Jews, has actually allowed herself to be stuffed into the lips and throat of Prince Albertross, the popular and majestic owner of the splendid sand mansion, and at least one half a quarter of an acre of Saline ground, called, known, and designated upon the map as " Coney Island Point."

The officers of the household of the fair bride began to arrive at Fulton Market, at one quarter before six o'clock, A. M.—looking very sleepy and very hungry. The Alderman of the 18th Ward, the Head Justice of the Police Office, the Lord Chamberlain of the Marine Court, Archbishop Shad, his Grace the Duke of Mackerel, the Duke of Rigmarole, his Honor Daniel O'Lobster, the High Constable, Prince Philorugglesius, Chancellor Blackhawk, Lord What-a-licking, Sir Loin, Sir Beefsteak, Sir Cutlet, Sir Calveshead, the Lords in Waiting, the Ladies in Waiting, Maids of Honor— *made* to see every thing done *Honor* bright—Bedchamber women— we shall have to send to England to find out what they were intended for—Gentlemen-Rushers, Loafers, Bearon-s, Counts, No-ac-counts, and all the rest of the invited part of heaven-created nobility, assembled at precisely six.

The Ladies of Miss Saussage's suite were summoned by the Master of the horses that were to drag them, at about one-quarter past six. We say *about*, because we are in extreme doubt in reference to the seconds, although we have made the most painful exertions to arrive at the precise moment. The Ladies all jumped upon the carts with extreme grace, amid the enthusiastic plaudits of the assembled multitude, which had now lined the streets, and rendered the progress of the carts and their interesting contents difficult, if not dangerous. Mrs. O'BLESSINGTON was particularly remarked for the fulness of her bust, and the liveliness of her action, and the delicious freedom of the favors which she bowed to the common people.

At half past six the suit of the happy ALBERTROSS mounted their carts under a heavy discharge of two pistols, and the roll of a bass drum. Notice was immediately afterwards given to the happy bridegroom, that it was time for him to begin to get his heart into the proper state of palpitation, and to prepare for family duty.

The Royal Locofoco Bridegroom immediately quitted the retiring room of the fish-stall, where he had been feverishly reposing, and passed through the market in the uniform of a private militia corporal, with plate and feather. We took notice, with great pleasure, that he showed his American contempt for " orders," by wearing his pantaloons in great *disorder*, and that his stockings were bound by no *garters*,

He wore the insignia of a First High Priest of the order of *night-hood*, and the star of the order of *Bosom Comesir*. The alderman of the 18th Ward was decorated with a stick mounted with a piece of *real-gilt*. The head Justice appeared in his usual official robes——having, out of his modesty and meekness, long since adopted, and steadfastly held fast to,'the example of culprits whom he has converted——an apparel consisting of a great-coat that had been through the hands of seven pawnbrokers, for improvement, highly embellished with *cuts* and *engravings*, and splendidly furnished with *paint*ings, both of oil and water—we think we might safely add—gin. The grand Deputy Constabulator of the Police was dressed in a gorgeous suit of no-*fools cap*tion paper, on which were beautifully stamped the sections of the Revised Statutes of the State of New York relating to *Hush Money*. His Sea-green

Highness Archbishop Shad, was simply clad—being a Christian and the head of the Church—in his pontifical scales of silver, his salary being small.—The only ornament we noticed about his immaculate and sinless Glory, was a plain belt of diamonds, which his own apostolic incorruptibility had paid for out of the process of the pleasant tribute of his tythes, added to the donations of pious old women, and the tears of small children, whom his eloquence and proud description of the stars in Heaven had caused to cry. The Duke of Mackerel was arrayed in a superb dress of *net* work, brought from *Fish-herland*, expressly for this purpose. The Hon. Dan. O'Lobster appeared in the dress of a water-Field Marshall, red and black, with claws, each with a penny " *passant*," tongue-armed and *ling*ued, with teeth azure, a duplinected portrait of *Erinnys* and Cataline being painted upon his patriotic back.

But enough. Time wastes, and we are anxious to give the first intelligence. We wish to be, as usual in advance of all the other papers. We have no moment left to tell the color of the ladies' frocks, and petticoats, and. chemisettes ; we can barely say that they all showed their noble blood, particularly the butcher's wives, in and out. There was no mistaking them for anything but women—republican queens—and while it may be said that they do not belong to English *no-a-bility*, we are sure, from the tremendous and exulting upshoutings of the crowd as they successively made their appearance, that they are set down in the hearts of all people who agree with them as individuals of the greatest *Ability*.

The procession was formed at precisely one minute and a quarter after seven. The prince rode in a wheelbarrow, drawn by two mules, each led by the head by a New Orleans negro. It was remarked that as the bridegroom got into the barrow, he was very pale, and he showed his characteristic humanity and urbanity by condescendingly asking one of the negroes if he was sure the mules' ears were on tight. On imbibing a gin cocktail, brought to him by an equerry, who was coming from Holt's-hotel-palace with a load of wood, the Prince seemed to be much relieved, and he sat up straight, just like any common man. He held the glass in his own hands, and drank with his own mouth. Nothing seemed to disturb the happy serenity of his countenance, although we regret to say that there was a slight tumor on his nose, and the fading remains of a scratch across his eyebrow—both, however, trophies of his early piety, and valor in battle. The procession now moved towards the Fulton Ferry, preceded by a squadron of Lynchers. The Directors of that valuable Ferry, with their natural and praiseworthy spirit of accommodation, had taken early pains to stop the flood tide from coming in, and had banked out the river across, from side to side, by ramparts and bastions of Graham bread—*lapis durus*—so as to make a splendid crossing place over which the company might go without wetting a single hub of their wheels. The bottom was hard, and beautifully variegated with the bones of different-dead fish, men, &c. It was happily observed by the Prince that the floor was truly *Mosaic.* This delightful sally, on being communicated to the gentlemen and ladies on the carts, produced such a roar of laughter that the Ferry-master himself felt bound to send a little boy to the Prince, to solicit him to stop his wit, or else the *cortege* would laugh down the abutments of the river, and get the whole party *foaming.* The Prince replied with his usual good nature, that he agreed that *Attic salt* was better than *East River* salt, and in the most affable manner desired the lad to say to his employer he would not let the party get into liquor of any kind by means of his own invitation, or compulsion, until they arrived at Brooklyn Heights, where the marriage was to be solemnized. We are happy to add that the Ferry-master expressed great gratification on the receipt of this pleasing intelligence, and dispatched an answer to Prince Albertross by a clam-boy, who had just sold out, full of meek acknowledgment of the gracious condescension of the Prince. The happy train then passed over in the following order—

First Cart ;—Two Gentlemen Rushers—Janitor of St. Catharine-slip College—Groom of the Centreville Course.

Second Cart ;—Equerry in waiting, Hon. Your Grandfather—Two Pages of Honor, with indexes on their faces—Groom in waiting, holding a brush and a horse-towel.

Third Cart ;—Clerk of the market—High Constable—Superintendent of Streets—the Hon. Aleck Niger, President of the Court of Dover—Clam-boy in waiting.

Fourth Cart ;—Bedchamber women in waiting, in a dreadful hurry—Captain of the *Ewe-man* Guard, Earl Ram—" *Master of the Buckhounds,*" Captain Florida—"*Treasurer of the Household,*" Lord Swartwout.

Fifth Cart ;—Maid of Honor in waiting—Duchess of Pretension's Lady in waiting, Lady Susan Dountous—" Gold Stick," Lord Astor—Lord in waiting, Viscount Poverty—Devil a-waiting, Lord Sinner.

Sixth Cart ;—Lady of the Chamber furniture in waiting, Hon. Miss Empty—Master of the Horses and Mules, Lord Ostler—Lord Steward, Earl of Abyssinia, Lord Chamberlain, the Earl of Hugbridget.

Seventh Cart—Miss Saussage all alone by herself, it being considered the most impressive style of doing the thing to ride her separate and apart, not only from her husband, but

even from her mother and intimate friends.   This superiority
of taste and more delicate refinement was generally remarked
as being highly to the advantage of American propriety, and
far exceeding that of the fashion prevailing in some foreign
parts.

Eighth Cart—ALBERTROSS in his wheel barrow, brought
up the rear, in the manner above described.

The party arrived at Brooklyn Heights, at three minutes
and fifty-nine seconds and one quarter after eight o'clock, and
soon put up a magnificent pavilion of oiled-cloth, under the
shade of a most thalamical looking grove of pines, which had
been for some time past under cultivation for the purpose.
The solemn ceremonies proceeded without the slightest delay.
The bridegroom after affectionately *kissing the hand !* of the
mother of his betrothed, so audibly that some of the ladies
present actually fainted, led the sweet Miss Saussage to a
rock where Archbishop Shad was standing, book in hand to
read the couple into glory.   We are pleased to repeat the observation common in every person's mouth, that he did it most
efficaciously ;—not a word of the service was omitted.   In
addressing the members of this new partnership of flesh, he
even called them by their *Christian* names—*Molusca* and
Albertross.   The bridegroom endowed the bride with all his
worldly goods, [the inventory of which is at present mislaid]
the vows were spoken—allegiance—fidelity—love—truth—
honor—*obedience !*—necessity—nature—nurses, and all the
other pathetic and thrilling incidents of a *real love match* were
mixed up together, and overwhelmed us so that we hastily
retired with a sort of jealous grief to leave the tied couple
together.

We conclude our hasty report by adding that we are assured by the highest authority that the bridegroom's linen was

made by a highly distinguished manufacturing house in the
county of Connaught, and that he has no corns.   At the time
we left the solemn process of annexation, it was confidently
believed that the happy parties would actually go to bed together at night.   The wedding cake was a monster of beauty,
being made by that distinguished *cuisinier* Thomas Downing,
Esq., of Broad Street.   It was manufactured out of three
hundred of the best salted codfish, compounded with five hundred bushels of potatoes from the farm of Sir Skin Kidney,
and fifteen kegs of Goshen butter.   Further particulars in our
next.

P. S. We omitted to mention that on the next morning the
republican Queen Molusca and the happy Albertross were
observed sitting upon the dock below the berth occupied by
the Providence steamboats, looking cool, fresh, and vigorous,
and reading *the last number of the " Spirit of the Times."*

VIEW OF NEW YORK FROM BEDLOW'S ISLAND.

If any man would be melancholy and patriotic, let him
take a seat, of a sunny afternoon, upon the old ramparts of
Bedlow's Island, and gaze and meditate.   Not that melancholy and amorpatriæ are natural associates, visiting people
with their spirit, in company ; may we never laugh again on
the fourth of July if we intended to say such a thing.   But
we are bold to declare, that no gentleman of reasonable taste
and tenderness of heart, can lean against that solitary fort,

16*

and drink in the ocean air playing around it, and lose his eyes in the blue sky above it, without being lulled into unquestionable pensiveness. We are further confident to assert that no scene-hunting American can look upon the panorama that encircles him, when he stops the sweep of his oar and backs water ten yards off from that island, and not swell with pride that this is his bay, and that is his city, and that his country is the most beautiful, and the freest, and the happiest in the world. Try it. Ye, whose dyspeptic grief paints everything in mournful colors, take an oar in your hand on the first April day when the sweet south-west shall gently blow in the face of Sol. Try it.

That the artist who painted the picture which draws out this commentary, felt the power of the scene when he sketched it, his success well warrants us to believe. One might get the bay, and harbor, and suburbs of New York by heart, by studying this engraving. First, on your north lies Gibbet Island—barren rock—sacred to the rope of the hangman. The smoke of a steamboat-pipe, to the west, indicates the watery turnpike which Duch frows of English Neighborhood travel over, bringing grateful offerings in spring time, fresh eggs and horse-radish, to Washington-market. Next Paulus Hook stands revealed, of which nothing better can be said than that it was whilom the country-seat of " the honorable, wise and prudent William Kieft, director-general of New Netherland," and that he sold it in May, 1638, to Abraham Planck, for four hundred and fifty guilders. Abraham leased it to Gerrit Derkson for a tobacco plantation. But the estate is now out of the family. The glory of the Dutch is departed ! —Further on, we catch a glimpse of the tall cliffs of Weehawken ; Weehawken, glorious in the sublime gloom of mountain crags and solemn trees—wet with the blood of

Hamilton—honored in the verse of Halleck. The Palisades next faintly show their ragged precipices, and by their side runs the river of rivers, bearing to his far source the luxuries and comforts of foreign commerce. How beautifully distinct is that scarcely visible fleet of sloops, fading, as it were, gradually away, until they seem to be only the white wings of floating sea-fowl, hovering over schools of *mummy-chubs*, and dipping up the scholars for their dinners. Turn, now, northeast. There is your American London. There is your city of five-hundred oyster-shops. This is the emporium of steamboats and liberty poles. There is the heart of politics, commerce, piety, and all manner of iniquity. But who is not proud of this city? Who can look upon its lofty spires, its forests of masts piercing the sky, its tribute-bearing sea-servants crossing its bay and traversing the world, to add to its wealth and honor,

> " Nor feel the prouder of his native land ?"

What is more beautiful than the sunny waters of the East River, as they run by the frowning castle on Governor's Island—castle more terrible upon paper than in its crumbling, rotten stone! Follow it up toward the Sound. Can you believe that such a pleasant stream is the road to Hell-gate? Here sentimental gentlemen may moralize a little. Cross to Brooklyn, and your eye rests upon a young queen, beginning to be a sister city. With our little sister we will shut our eyes. We will contemplate the picture no more. We have seen glory enough.

There is only one other of the several cities that gem our bay, which we miss from the delineation before us. Does not the reader's spirit sigh with ours, when we tearfully whisper, *Communipaw!* But that city is behind us, reader, and shares the sublimity of invisibility with the Narrows and

the ocean.   But there, industriously toiling in that boat, are the
representatives of the ancient Dutch fish emporium.   Yes, doubtless, those gentleman are the members from Communipaw.
You might know it from the characteristic grasp of the oys-
ter-tongs in the hands of the one, and from the sable com-
plexion of the other ; only there is a cast of mournful thought
upon the brow of the last, and he does not grin and show his
teeth, as hath been the fashion of Communipaw negroes from
the time whereof the memory of man knoweth not, etc.   Perhaps he hath had bad luck.   " Delightful task !" as the poet
says, to scrape and poke all day, that Downing's reputation
as an oyster-caterer may be honored, and the rakers and
scrapers in adjoining Wall-street be made fat !   We pause
for the sake of admiration.

    Two hundred years ago !   That was not much in the times
of the patriarchs.   It is nothing absolutely wonderful now—
only the length of life of two old people.   And yet in those
two hundred years what changes have taken place !   The
wilderness has become a city !   Nations have been extir-
pated !   Nothing has remained but the sea, and the everlasting air.   The sea still laves the shore, but it is a shore peopled with dock-rats, instead of being overhung with foliage
and flowers.   The air still plays upon the island of Manhattan ; but, instead of the perfume of roses and sweet fruits,
caught up in green lanes and pleasant groves, it is pregnant
with pepper and snuff in South-street, and driving limestone
dust in Broadway.   All, all is changed.   It is worse than
was to Rip Van Winkle the transformation of jolly King
George's rubicund face into the buff and blue of General
Washington.   Only one resemblance in the physico-moral
world remains.   Two hundred years ago the " savages" would

have scalped you; the modern savages of Gotham only shave you.

Two hundred years hence! O prophecy! we cannot bear to listen to thee. We will only dare to hope that we may live to see the year 2000, and that our lots on One hundredth-street may then be worth principal and interest.

THE RIGHT USE OF SILVER.

[From the New York Commercial Advertiser, April 1, 1837.]

OUR sheet is not half large enough to contain all that we should like to put in it every day, and were it twice as large as it is, still we should have to struggle daily with the inconveniences of too narrow limits—desires expanding, as in most other matters, with the means of giving them indulgence. Therefore the appropriation of a column to any one subject, is at all times a trial of our virtue. But we would rather exclude a column of our own choicest handiwork, than omit the subjoined report of certain doings at Hempstead, on Saturday the 25th ultimo; and the rather for it has not been forced upon us by a request for publication, but fallen accidentally into our hands, without even a hint of its existence, or of the proceedings which it describes. We copy it from the Long Island Star, in which we discovered it yesterday by the merest chance, while looking over the outside columns. The presentation address is one of the happiest we have ever read, and the reply perfect—exactly what might have been expected from the lips of the brave old man who uttered it.

On Saturday last a peculiarly interesting scene was presented at Hempstead, in Queens county. A committee of gentlemen from the fifth ward, New York, appointed a meeting with Raynor R. Smith, at the Hotel of Mr. Oliver Conklin for the purpose of presenting him a token of regard from the citizens of that ward.

At four o'clock in the afternoon, the gentlemen from New York arrived, and the presentation took place in the presence of a number of people. The hardy mariner received the compliments bestowed upon him with much modesty, and after the public ceremonies were over, withdrew into a private room with a few friends, where hilarity warmed into confidence, and he was led to recount a number of the "hair-breadth scapes" which form part of the business of the life of a wrecker at Rockaway. The mode in which he related the rescue of Capt. Nathan Holdredge,—the individual referred to in the address below—from the jaws of death, made a vivid impression upon all present. Nature and truth gave power of language beyond the refinements of the pen.

After a cheerful interview of two or three hours, the company separated with warm expressions of mutual regard

We give below the address of William P. Hawes, Esq., on presenting the cup, together with Mr. Smith's reply.

ADDRESS OF W. P. HAWES.

MR. RAYNOR R. SMITH.—We are a committee, appointed by the citizens of the fifth ward of the city of New York, to discharge the difficult task of expressing to you their admiration of

your chivalrous attempt to rescue the passengers and crew of
the barque Mexico, lately stranded on the adjacent beach,
and to ask your acceptance of a trifling token of their regard for your intrepidity. You, sir, cannot have forgotten
the terrors of that distressful wreck, nor is it possible for us
not to remember, how nobly you and your gallant associates
adorned humanity, and how well you redeemed our coast
from the ignominy of inhospitality. Having waited, in vain,
for the recognition of your services in a more general and
distinguished manner, we have felt that we owe it to our
city—to the credit of our country—so far as in our power
lies, to express to you the sentiments we entertain of your
perilous adventure. We cannot forget the morning of that
eventful day, when the weary Mexico, with an insufficient
and mutinous crew, doomed to unavoidable destruction, poured
out her signal guns of distress among the breakers of Long
Island—when mothers and sisters, and children and rough
sailors stretched imploring hands to the shore, and screamed
unavailing prayers to Him who rules the storm ; when, as
if to turn into mockery the attempt to save the predestined
ship, He gave violence to the winds and fury to the waves,
and builded between the vessel and the shore a wall of
floating ice, which scarce even hope itself could struggle to
surmount. Who that saw, or has heard, can ever forget
the scene—The lingering death of a hundred martyrs to
cold, and hunger, and hope disappointed—freezing in the
sight of comfortable hearths—starving in the view of abundance—despairing in the midst of promise ! I cannot attempt
to paint a description of that day and night of horror !

> " Enclosed with all the demons of the main,
>   They viewed the adjacent shore, but viewed in vain ;
>   Such torments in the drear abode of Hell,
>   Where sad despair laments with rueful yell,

"Such torments agonize the damned breast.
While fancy views the mansions of the blest ;
For Heaven's sweet help their suppliant cries implore,
But Heaven relentless deigns to help no more."

It was amid the terrors of such a scene, when the boldest and the skilfullest stood upon the beach in doubt, and dismay, and awe, that risking every thing but honor, and the praise of the humane, your sole adventurous skiff struggled through the resisting ice, and climbed the overwhelming mountains of surf, and sought to bring salvation to the perishing wretches who ought to have expected rather to receive you as a fellow sufferer, rather than to welcome you as a saviour. What Heaven denied to their prayers, it seemed willing to grant to your courage. Eight souls live to pray for the future reward of your exertions. The rest cold death claimed for his portion. Had it been possible that they might have been saved, had it been permitted that another one should be rescued, we know that you were the brave deliverer who would have plunged into the gulph for his redemption. The city knows the fact—the commercial and christian world applaud the heroism of your endeavors.

Such conduct has in other countries, gained for less daring heroes the reward of civic crowns and national honors. He who saved the life of a Roman was honored with a seat next to the senate, and public assemblies when he entered, rose to do him reverence. These rewards we cannot give you. But such as your fellow countrymen can give, of gratitude to one who has rendered honor to the state, such we bestow. These we yield—these we bring in tribute. That your children, and the children of your brave boys, may not complain that Americans cannot appreciate acts of devotion, and danger, and that your distant posterity may have preserved among them the glorious example of their ancestor, we have caused a skilful artist to engrave upon silver a faint sketch of your achievement. Upon this cup, which I now tender for your acceptance, is embossed the story of the Mexico, and the glory of Raynor R. Smith. It is but a sketch, for the labors of the artist, however successful, can imitate only the prominent features of the scene. Here, it is true, lies the ill fated vessel groaning in the deep sand—the freezing water rushing through her broken timbers, and over her shattered spars, and her shrouds swinging with hope-abandoned wretches. Here has the graver pictured your wished-for boat, and we can see the steady helm, and the strong nerved sinewy pull of the oars that bear her through the surge. But the howling storm—the viewless wind bearing upon its wings the chill of death—the cries of the victims—your own encouraging shout of comfort, giving strength and confidence to your crew—what mortal could engrave them? Imagination must supply what human art cannot pretend to depict.

In tendering to you, sir, this token of our regard, we do not expect greatly to add to your honor, nor to increase the esteem in which you must be held by every man who appreciates virtuous heroism. It is, perhaps, more as a relief to our own hearts, than as a sufficient tribute to your merits, that we bring our offering. Justice to ourselves requires us, nevertheless, to say it is not a mere impulse, not an emotion springing from the first impression produced by the performance of a good action, that has prompted this expression of our feelings. This memorial has been considered. The worthiness of your conduct has been weighed. It is from deliberate justice, as well as from glowing admiration, that our tribute springs.

We cannot forbear upon this occasion, to add an expres-

sion of our feeling toward your associates in the enterprise
which we celebrate, and to render a just acknowledgment
to the humanity and kindness of the people of Hempstead.
In many foreign lands, such hospitalities to the saved, and
such pious solemnities to the lost, would never have been
rendered. The sailor poet of old England, from whose experience I have already quoted, speaks of

> " A lawless brood,
> On England's vile inhuman shores who stand,
> The foul reproach and scandal of the land,
> To rob the wanderer wrecked upon the strand."

It is a subject of painful regret that even some parts of our
own shores have not been free from the barbarities of the
Picaroon. But the coast of Long Island is happily purged
from the disgrace. The home-seeking packet ship, and the
storm-beaten merchantman, hereafter looking upon the hills
of Long Island, will bear in comfortable remembrance as they
bear away from its lee shore, that should all human endeavors fail, and they be driven upon the strand, you and your
good example live here, and the Long Islanders are charitable and kind. The merchants of the great commercial emporium may perhaps have cause to attribute it to the humanity
of the inhabitants of the sea side, more than to the activity of
our pilots, that commerce shall continue to spread her multi-
tudinous sails toward the harbor of New York.

Permit me, now, in conclusion, to express the gratification
which I personally feel in being the organ of expression of
the sentiments of our constituents. None can know better
than I know, how well this tribute is bestowed. I have had
the enjoyment of your acquaintance for many years and have
witnessed more than one instance of your skill, and courage.
I have partaken of your hospitality in the islands of the sea,
and have had good occasion to commend the staunchness of

your surf boat. But there lives a worthy citizen who will commend, more than I know how to do, the intrepidity which is the theme of our present praise. Years since, at the imminent peril of your own life, you rescued Captain Nathan Holdredge from the surf, and recalled him from the jaws of death back to grateful life For him and for all the other citizens whom you have saved to the republic, we thank you. And we pray that your valuable life may long be spared, if not to act in future cases of distress, to teach and encourage your sons and grandsons how to win esteem on earth, and a worthy welcome into Heaven.

REPLY OF RAYNOR R. SMITH.

GENTLEMEN—I thank you, I sincerely thank you for your gift. In return for it I can only say that should a similar wreck or any other wreck ever again occur on our shores, I shall endeavor to show that I deserve it. I shall preserve your gift. I shall value it above all price—it shall remain with me while I live, and when I die it shall not go out of my family, if I can help it.

DESCRIPTION OF THE CUP.

The cup bears on the one side a device of the ship Mexico imbedded in the sand, with the waves breaking over her. Her hapless crew is seen stretching out their imploring hands. A boat is making its way to them. A few figures stand upon the beach, surrounded by masses of ice, which show the severity of the season, and the peril of the undertaking.

The reverse side bears the following inscription :

REWARD OF MERIT.

Presented to Raynor R. Smith, of Hempstead South, L. I.

by a number of his fellow citizens of the Fifth Ward, as a token of regard for his noble daring, performed at the peril of his life, in saving the eight persons from the wreck of the fated *Ship Mexico*, on the morning of January 2d, 1837.

NEW YORK.

Committee.—Joseph Meeks, John Horspool, Lawrence Ackerman, William Kelley, Benjamin Ringgold, William P. Hawes.

CASTLE GARDEN.

THE time is now, when middle aged citizens say to their wives and daughters, as they stand twenty-five yards this side of the gate-way opening to the castle bridge, " I remember the time when this was the west barrier of the battery, and from here, and close along the old flag-staff house, famous for oranges and peanuts, down to the old long wharf, at Whitehall, ran a frail, trembling fence, of white painted pine. Here, on the north side of the bridge, indulged boys—too happy—and weary cashiers and clerks, when the tide served, threw out their heavy-sinkered lines for bass and weak fish, and drew rich suppers from the propitious Hudson, then un-vexed by steamboats. Here on the left, were the ferry stairs. Many a man of us was a boy then, and, on Saturday after-noon's vacation, excused his return after sundown, by a string of begauls, and occasional blackfish, caught from the steps of that ancient ferry. But it is all gone now. The ferry and the fish have departed.

We have heard and seen such good citizens sigh, and shake

their heads in melancholy. Such is the inevitable bitterness of population and improvement. But how will it be ten, or five years hence? The world, especially the First Ward of it, does not lie still. Here we have had forts and breastworks pulled down and levelled, and the *battery* turned into a pleasure ground, and the river encroached upon, and old Hudson actually submitting to King Canute's law, and a war castle put up, and then turned into a hall of music and fireworks, and every thing changed—all, all in a believable time.

Must we expect no more change?

Reader, get that piece of silver changed at the very enticing banking house, at the arch way, and get one of Marsh's tickets instead, and then cross the bridge with me, and see. How swiftly rushes flood-tide beneath the arches of these piers! How comfortable the sensation of safety from the whirlpools beneath your feet, as you lean over the railing, and look into the black water? Yet a decree has gone forth that all this shall be changed. Time, as well as heavy horse, and light footed maidens, has galloped over this bridge, and has shaken the stones, and loosened the iron, and rotted the woodwork. The worshipful Mayor and Council, not to be behind time, are devising how soon the water shall be dammed out and the castle and the bridge be both demolished; and the lovers of the sublime and beautiful in Wall street and Exchange place are feasting their imaginations with goodly rows of store-houses fringing the river side, and already seem to hear instead of Marsh's orchestra raising a Pæan to the Gods, the deep *yoheho* of niggers hoisting skins and indigo to the fourth story!

Every man, woman, and child that does not now and then take a walk on the battery and then cross the bridge, and enter the fort-garden, and mount to the topmost promenade on

17*

the walls, and purify his soul in the winds that are permanently engaged for the establishment, will lament ere long *the change* which will bring destruction to the pleasures which are now afternoonly enjoyed by the Deputy

Inspector of the First Ward.

[From the New York Times of October 28, 1834.]

My dear, good Times——That was a sinister sort of waggish suggestion of yours, to the Commercial the other day ; that it was not doing even-handed justice, to stick a motto along side of Seward's name, and leave Stillwell——"the interesting" Mr. Stillwell——all——"alone in his glory." The Colonel might have answered you, and showed his learning, if he had a mind, and had, moreover, read Beaumont and Fletcher. How he might have swamped you with his quotation from " The false One." How he might have glorified himself, and his candidate, by halo-ing it around the Lieutenant-Governor's patronymic !

> CÆSAR.   " Not a man, Antony,
> That were to show our fears and dim our greatness :
> No—'Tis enough ! MY NAME'S ASHORE !"

But the Colonel knows more about Anti-Masonry, and Militia tactics, than he does about joking, and dead poets ; and so he thanked you kindly for the hint, and stuck in an extract from a letter *said to have been* written by Stillwell, which contained " the interesting" information that certain things were *going to be done*, which *had been done already.* The author of that document, and the time of its composition, have *not yet* been discovered. There the extract stands, though, and the Colonel—I suppose—made the best selection that his reading, and the source of collation, could provide. Now, every body knows that Stillwell did not concoct, or " get up," that idea. No man in his senses can believe it.

" Stop thief, stop thief," is sounded in the streets, and a bold faced larcener feels the fingers of a sturdy democrat in his neck. Pilfered citizens come up and claim their apparel, with which the rascal has adorned himself. He is stripped —restitution is made, though justice not yet done—his jewels, watch, rings, coat, hat, boots, jacket—all, all are claimed and identified, and delivered to their proper owners. Nothing remains but his pantaloons and shirt. Will the presumption be that these are " original ?" Should he happen to have a horse with him, will any man doubt that he has committed a plagiarism upon that " interesting" animal ? The Col. must take and feel the force of this allegory. If he does not, I pray you, elucidate, indoctrinate him. Tell him, moreover, that the sentiment which he has selected, is not apposite, nor appropriate, and give him the following to select from. These are respectable, honest, genuine quotations. Since Stillwell must have a motto, let him have one that is somewhat relative to his character and talent.

A FRIEND OF MODEST MERIT.

" Quid domini facient, *audent cum talia fures !*"
Virg. Ecl. 3. 16.

" It is a greater offence to steal men's labors, than their clothes." *Synesius.*

" The character of men may be known from the company they keep. The receiver is as bad as the thief."
Burton's Anat. Melancholy.

" Stop that man—stop that man !"

The Literary Larcener.

" There was one old gentleman in a claret colored coat,
with a lean, pale, solemn expression of countenance, who had
all the appearance of a broken down lawyer making a brief
for a speech at a club meeting.   After considering him atten-
tively, I recognized in him a diligent getter up of miscella-
neous works and political tracts, that bustled very well off
with the trade.   I was curious to see how he manufactured
his wares.   He made more stir and show of business than
any one of the others ; dipping into various books, fluttering
over the leaves of manuscripts, taking a morsel out of one, a
morsel out of another, " line upon line, precept upon precept,
here a little and there a little."   The contents of his book
seemed to be as heterogeneous as those of the witches caul-
dron in Macbeth.   It was here a finger, and there a thumb,
toe of frog and blind worm's sting, with his own gossip poured
in like " baboon's blood" to make the medley " slab and good."

Sketch Book.

" If the boy steal adroitly, give him credit ; but, if he be
detected in a plagiarism, lick him."   Lycurgus.

" When I see a barrister defending and eulogizing a palpable criminal, I cannot help asking my brethren on the bench,
whether his license had not better be taken away."—Lord
Mansfield's charge to the jury in Filchet's case.

" Ton d' apameibomenos prosephe cry—own thatu stoleit."

Homer's Iliad

" Bring me no more reports."   Richard 3d.

" Blitzer vongallowsboots tutite foghris footerno."

Schleigzel.

" Pero caballero, ymd debe saber que aunque un tacano no

es un ladron, la diferencia entre un tacano quien recibe sin pagar los bienes robados de su vecindad, y un ladron quien los roba es diferencia de poco momento."

Lazarillo de Tormes.

Y por eso se llama el hombre quien roba con talento, en nuestro Castellano " *El Robador Experimentado,*" en Frances " *Le Voleur Parfait,*" en Italiano, " *Il Ladro Astuto,*" y en Ingles *Steal-well.*"

Quevedo El Gran Tacano.

" E giusto il vostro sdegno
 Qui vi sono de ladri—Examiniamo
 Processiamo."

La Gazza Ladra.

" Ah birba, birba
 Ecco la sul ponte, oh se potessi
 Arrampicarmi."

La Gazza Ladra.

" Vous m'accusez d'etre voleur—Vous me condamnez, et peut être je serai pendu, et qu'est ce que j'ai fait ? l'avais besoin d' un chapeau, et j'ai mis mes mains sur le chapeau de mon voisin, un chapeau dont il n'avait pas besoin, et pour lequel il a donne peut être deux piastres. Et mon très honorable juge, vous avez vole les idées de vos amis ; vous avez publie des livres dans lesquels, il n'y est pas une idèe originale, pas meme une expression qui n'appartient pas a vos amis— Mais c'est un emprunt avec vous, et moi je suis voleur selon vos regles de justice. Oh juge sage, eclairè, honorable."

Causes Celebres—vol 35, p. 79.

" Wyauarchysox haughhiho gibletxg worryworrywo."

Black Hawk's Address to General Atkinson.

" Hong hien long grit fuz ! hong, hang, hung."—*Confucius.*

" Who steals my brains, steals trash." *Longworth.*

" The receivers of property embezzled, knowingly, are subject to the same punishment as the thief."
                                        Revised Statutes.

" And be it further enacted, that in all cases of theft, larceny, or robbery, which shall come before the court of errors aforesaid, for trial, judgment, or direction, and the members of the said court shall be divided thereon ; the defendant shall not be sent either to Auburn or Sing Sing, unless the Lieut. Governor, presiding in said court, shall under seal, certify that he does not know a case of a man untried, who in the eye of God, and of common morality, is a worse thief than the prisoner at the bar.   *do.*

P. S. I asked my lawyer to give me some authorities touching the liability of people who endorse their friends reputation, but he would not do it. " Pshaw !" said he, " the endorser is equally liable with the drawer. If, when a man has found his visitor to be a rogue, he does not kick him out of doors, his *honest* friends will quit his house, and cut him."
                              A FRIEND, &C.

[From the New York Times of November 10, 1834.]

MESSRS. EDITORS.—If I remember rightly, the wigs promised to give it up, if they lost this election—this one, at which they had the majority of the inspectors, and all the lamplighters on their side. Now, will they do it ? Will they submit to the expression of the will of the majority ?

Or will they follow their *ignis fatuus* leader, and be tumbled again into the swamps and bogs of bad temper and lost bets? Some of them will not, I know. In fact, I believe that the majority of the opposition in this city, are sensible of the blind captivity into which they have been led by their editorial prophet. But Hark! the trumpet is blown! the tocsin is sounded! to the rescue! is the cry! war to the knife! says the Courier of Saturday. "Let us rally, and organize, draw the line between us and the democrats, distinctly; let us employ no man, love no woman, own no friend, who thinks not with us; nor counsel, nor cure, nor feed, nor clothe, nor buy from, nor speak to any individual, high or low, rich or poor, kinsman or stranger, whoever he may be, unless he throws up his hat and hurras for wiggery. That is the substance of it. Look at the manifesto—the fiat—the imperial decree. With what a pompous consequence, the dictator issues his this "*must*" be done, and that "*must*" be done. However, there is no use of quarrelling about these things. Rather let us laugh at them, and show their utter absurdity. With this view I have been tumbling over the first book of Paradise Lost. That is a book, by the bye, which they who mean to "take courage from despair," ought to read, The Courier has drawn from it already.

> "———What though the field be lost?
> All is not lost, *the unconquerable will*
> *And study of revenge, immortal hate*
> *And courage never to submit, or yield,*
> Or what is else not to be overcome."

That was what Satan said to his next door neighbor when he turned over upon his aching side, in the current of hot stuff, into which he and his followers had been lately plunged, after being defeated in a hard fought battle. What a prototype of the general-in-chief of the wigs. "Never give it up," he cries. Fight for spite's sake, and hate and revenge. Banish them from your families, and friendships, hold no communion with them, proscribe them as outlaws.—And then he reasons. How *devilish* plausible !

> " Since, through experience of the great event,
> In arms not worse, in foresight much advanced
> We may, with more successful hope, resolve
> To wage by force, or guile, eternal war,
> Irreconcilable to our grand foe,
> Who now triumphs, and in the excess of joy
> Sole reigning, holds the tyranny of Heaven.
> So spake the apostate angel, though in pain,
> Vaunting aloud, but racked with deep despair."

And so speaks, and vaunts " the apostate" dictator of the wigs. " We are," says he, " in arms not worse ;" that is to say, we've got all the talent and decency on our side, and the control of the city treasury ; —" in foresight much advanced ;" that is to say, we know, now, that we cannot reckon upon our own honesty. There have been traitors among us—But let Milton speak. In the following extract, one would think he was describing a tribulation meeting at Masonic Hall.

> " All these, and more came flocking, but with looks
> Downcast, and dark, yet such wherein appeared
> Obscure some glimpse of joy, to have found their chief
> Not in despair, to have found themselves not lost
> In loss itself, which on his countenance cast
> Like doubtful hue ; but he, his wonted pride
> Soon recollecting, with high words, that bore
> Semblance of worth, not substance, gently raised
> Their fainting courage, and dispelled their fears."

I beg to be understood, as quoting these passages with no intentional irreverence, with no spirit of exultation over, or taunt against the many respectable well meaning individuals that compose the main body of the wigs. I have made the quotations only to illustrate the devilish spirit of the counsel which the Courier gives to his defeated followers.

Since my hand is in, I'll give a few more illustrations.

The despirited legions, are at the call of their leader, met in Pandemonium. Satan *loquitur*.

> " ―――― And that strife
> Was not inglorious, though the event was dire,
> As this place testifies, and this dire change
> Hateful to utter."

In the same spirit the Courier would say, " we fought hard and did all that we could, although we got beat ; as the people—we have paid for steamboats, and frigates, and eagles, and liberty poles, and beer—will all testify, and also ' this dire *change*,' or cash, which we have got to hand over in payment of our bets."

> " But what power of mind
> Foreseeing or presaging, from the depth
> Of knowledge past or present, could have feared
> How such united force of Gods, how such
> As stood like these could ever know repulse !"

Just so reasons the Courier. The wigs have been taught to believe that they were the only wise and powerful people in the country. They believed in their invincibility. " Great reactions," they were told were going on in their favor, every where. Men were " breaking off by whole acres" from the democratic ranks. All H—l was moved to get up an excitement—and how could " such as stood like these," the great, the rich, the eloquent, the learned, and the cunning, get beat by Democrats. The style of reasoning is the same. There is a congenial sympathy between the two minds that is indeed most admirable. But Satan continues,

> " For who can yet believe, tho' after loss,
> That all these puissant legions, whose exile
> Hath emptied Heaven, shall fail to reascend
> Self-raised, and repossess their native seat.

" *Emptied Heaven*."—Arrogant vanity ! So the Courier talked when half a dozen lawyers joined his standard. And

mark the desperate presumption, which in the midst of rout
and discomfiture, aspires to future victories !

> " For me, be witness all ye host of Heaven,
> If counsels different, or dangers shunned
> By me, have lost our hopes."

Courier again.   Who believes that its shut up shop resolution or any other of its " counsels," were different, or disgusting to its party ?   And as to " shunning danger," look at
the bristling steel that invites the " hired bullies" to pay a visit
to the office !

After Satan had expressed his sentiments, then the other
leaders suggested their views as to the mode of carrying on
the war.   I will conclude with a short extract from the
speech of each.   Your readers can make the application.
Mammon addressed the meeting at length.

> " Mammon, the least erected spirit that fell
> From Heaven, for e'en in Heaven his looks and thoughts
> Were always downward bent."

He was for backing out entirely, and the substance of his
advice was,

> " Let us rather seek
> Our own good from ourselves, and from our own,
> *Live to ourselves.*"

Moloch—" My sentence is for open war, of wiles
> More unexpert, I boast not ; them let those
> Contrive, who need, or when they need not, use."

Belial—" I should be much for open war, O Peers,
> As not behind in hate, if what was urged,
> Main reason to persuade immediate war,
> Did not dissuade me most, and seem to cast
> Ominous conjecture on the whole success."

Beelzebub.—" Some advantageous act may be achieved,
> By sudden onset either with hellfire,
> To waste the whole creation, or possess
> All as our own, and drive, as we were driven,
> The puny habitants, OR IF NOT DRIVE,
> SEDUCE THEM TO OUR PARTY."

So counselled the fallen spirits, when they met " to reor-
ganize," in Pandemonium, as Milton, drawing from his
knowledge of bad hearts, powerfully imagines. Turn the
Courier's article of Saturday into blank verse, and you might
add it on to either of the speeches made at that meeting, and
no one could doubt its devilish origin.

POETICAL PARODIES.

18*

POETICAL PARODIES.

WATER.

AN ODE DEDICATED TO THE TEMPERANCE SOCIETY.

" Water is the best of elements."

WELL sung, and truly, thou old " bird of Jove,"
A proverb hast thou wove, for all good people ;
Arthur and I around the world might rove,
From high Acropolis to St. Paul's steeple,
Nor find such well epitomized sobriety,
To paint upon the flag of our society.

" Hoc signo vinces," Hale, unfurl the banner ;
Let it flaunt up, and flout the gin-swoln clouds ;
Shout now, a long, and clear, and bold Hosannah,
And herald life to the pale, Styx-like crowds,
Of " Five-points" wretches, dying ! by the Mass !
Of " the best of liquors, at three cents per glass !"

Not death, but life our bloodless triumphs yield,
Crowned with the joy of souls redeemed from slavery
But could we tempt the old jailor to the field,
There were a desperate fight for brother Avery—
Gods ! how he'd stamp his heel into his head,
And crush, even when the monster was stone dead ;

The dragon thief, that steals away men's brains ;—
Good Lot first cursed him, and vine-desser Noah ;
The brothel's god, e'er since, confessed he reigns,
Leading the nightly Bacchanalian roar.
Dread devil ! hear him chuckling at the banquet,
Say, wilt thou not a single gentleman quit ?

" The glasses sparkle on the board," and song,
And merry joke, and jest they wanton banter ;—
And he is there.   See, see him push along
With busy speed, the just refilled decanter ;
" Drink, drink boys, drink, and drown grim Care, and
   Sorrow,
Be drunk to night, and sober on the morrow."

The clock strikes three.   The gentle breath of morning
Fans the hot cheek of a zig-zag street walker ;
Why is that mud his spattered coat adorning ?
What dialect affects our late glib talker ?
Strange ! vest unbuttoned—pockets turned outside—
Hat pyramidical—soiled cravat untied !

These be thy half cooked dinners, old Constrictor,
Thy victims, ready buttered with saliva,
Soon to be mashed and munched, as in the picture
Of fated Laocoon—pained, fruitless striver ;
Have pity ! wretch !   Gloat not so on thy ration,
Or moderate, at least, thy tight *squassation.*

O, for the early days, that knew not art !
When, at the well, Bethuel's gentle daughter
Confessed her love, and pledged her virgin heart,
In a pure bowl of dimpling-cold spring water.

"Drink, drink my Lord," the maiden to the camel-dri-
ver said,
But not a drop she gave him that could get into his head.

And thou, Castalia, where is now thy fount,
Whose chrystal, erst, threw back young Poets' faces,—
Up, on the top of the Parnassian mount,—
The Muses' home, the loved haunt of the Graces ?
Is't true that Adrian filled thee up with stones ?
The drunken Vandal !   Curses on his bones !

Home of my fathers ! can I e'er forget
The pearly gem, set in thy sloping hill ?
The heated willows bending down, to wet
Their fanning branches in the pebbled rill ?
The swallow, o'er the mirror skimming—dipping—
And now and then a stray mosquito nipping ?

Oh water, wave, spring, rivulet, well, stream !
When art thou most the idol of my praise ?
Still art thou Castaly.—In sooth, I deem
Even Woodworth might a decent stanza raise,
Inspired by thee ;—yes, yes ;—I'll wage a ducat,—
Even he might feel the God, and sing some rotten bucket.

The diamond dripping from the brimming bowl,
The clear, deep streamlet, kissing its green sides,
The swelling river's proud and lordly roll,
Old ocean's bosom, and his rushing tides,
Rich sources are of holy contemplation ;—
Diviner, boasted not the famed old Roman nation.

Come ; enter this green lane ; the sun is hot ;——
Here shielded, thank the closely dove-tailed trees ;
Stoop, stoop, and drink——this is Egeria's grot.
Fall, man, upon thy bended hands, and knees,
And cool thy lip, and bless this happy minute——
Stay——wilt thou have " a little brandy" in it ?

No ! poison not the wholesome living streams,
Nor turn their waves, into the dead Red Sea,
Putrid with Pharoah's army ; where, it seems,
No bird may live, nor shrub or floweret be ;——
Where the chance pilgrim, thinks it providential,
If he survive the brazen sky, and simoon pestilential.

Oblivious are years, since Bacchus, flushed
With Chian, urged the lion-mated Tiger,
Impetuous ; and on to triumph rushed,
From farthest Ind to heavy rolling Niger ;
With syren, music, madness, thyrsus, cymbal,
Satyr, and Faun, Silenus, Pan, and vine wreathed pipe
          and timbrel,

A drunken multitude.   But times are changed ;
The insolvent God here claims no sacred shrines ;
Save, where by grateful Aldermen, are ranged
Long promised shambles, to retail " high wines."
O ! provident regard for cheap fruition !
Erin-nys staggering, thanks ye for the licensed imbibition.

Save, that in yonder secret Alms-house cellar,
The rusty key turns seldom, on that rare

Old private stock—from Lynch's—soft, and mellow,—
Peters can tell how long it ripened there.—
The rest of us all sip our thin Burgundy,
Abuse the booths, and preach reform, the coming anno
    mundi.

BANK MELODY—No. I.

A lament of a wig temperance man on being invited to the corporation
dinner on the 4th of July.

THE gushing wine is calling me,
With its merry, gleesome flow ;
And our party all are hauling me,
Where bright their glasses glow ;
I may not go, I must not go,
Where punch, pale ale, and sherry flow ;
Where flutenists and flowers blow ;—
    I must stay here with my wife and daughter,
    And sip the insipid Knapp's spring water ;—
Oh ! heavy life, wear on, wear on ;
That vow for me has the business done !

The sharp-set carver, through the round
Goes cutting, with its hungry sound ;
And over the blade spiced gravies flow
Into the steamy dish below ;
And fast and full the soup plates go
To Bull, Fred. Talmadge, and Munro ;

And all the way
They murmuring say
" Oh, fool! why thou art far away?
Come up to the City Hall to-day,
And with us the figure go."

I may not go, I may not go,
Where brilliant Hock's green waters run
All glided with reflected fun ;
Where leaps Champagne, from the bottle, below,
Into a whirl of boiling snow,
And the rabble gape as they see it go ;
    I must stay here
    In prison drear ;
Oh! heavy life, wear on, wear on ;
Would God that thou wert done !—

The fat head cook, good wig, goes by,
Arranging syllabub and viand,
And Sambo Ganymedes swift fly,
To help good fellows as get dry, and
Madeira makes them all rejoice,
And even old Hays with gentle voice,
    Calls me away,
    With the wigs to stay,
    To keep the day
    Which the Democrats say
Is their own blessed anniversary.

I may not go—I may not go,
Where the sweet winds over fresh salmon blow ;

Where the spicy pregnant clouds float by
The original Stillwell's dreamy eye ;
Nor where the soup, warm, rich, and black,
Runs gurgling 'mid the busy clack,
Like a sweet bird singing upon a hill,
To the splashing wheel of the village mill—
   I must stay here,
    With my wedded dear,
And munch roast clams like Cotton Mather,
And keep my vow to our good King Arthur.

O could I go, unknown, unseen,
And rapturous dip in the deep tureen,
And be the boy I would have been,
   But for that cursed vow !
Charles King and Root, and I and Noah,
Would make the old* Sessions ceiling roar,
And K——g get R——t upon the floor,
   " As drunk as David's sow."

BANK MELODY—No. II.

AIR—" Fallen is thy throne."

FALLEN is thy throne, O Nicholas !
   Silence is o'er thy Bank,
No more thy discounts tickle us,
   Thy lawyers all are lank.

* Vide the American of 1824.

Where are the boys that hanker,
  For notes approved and " done,"
Who vote for the old banker,
  Whenever they're hard run.

Clay ! thou did'st love Nick Biddle,
  Once he was all thine own ;
Thy harp, thy flute, thy fiddle
  Which thou did'st play upon ;
Till Jackson came and blighted
  Thy long loved olive tree,
And the Banking House was lighted,
  For other kings than thee.

Then sunk the sun of Nicholas,
  Then set his Evening Star,
And got into a pickle as
  Bad as Duane's papa,
When wrapped in wrath and wonder,
  He frowned upon his son,
And lectured him like thunder
  For what he had not done.

BANK MELODY—No. III.

AIR.—" Said a smile to a tear."

SAID Noah to Stone,
When the meeting was done,
And his heart bounded light as a feather,
While sipping his beer,
" In sooth, it is queer
That we should be both here together.

" I come here to thank
My good mistress, the bank,
For teaching me sound aristocracy."
" And I," said the Colonel,
" To curse the infernal
Old demon of Jackson democracy."

" O, ho !" chuckled Noah,
" Dear Stone say no more,
We are twins ; an't it wonderful funny ?
And how glorious the cause,
Which support from *us* draws
And fills both our pockets with money !"

BANK MELODY—No. IV.

Air.—Farewell! but whenever you welcome the hour."

["*To be sung by Mr. H-x-e, after the Election.*"]

FAREWELL ! but whenever you think of the hour
That gave to old Tammany honor and power,
Then think of the discounts, which we have had too,
And the loans, dearest Webster, we've made Clay, and you,
Our debts will press heavy ! no hope will remain !
And Nick will surrender his office with pain !
But he ne'er will forget the free discounts, that threw
Their enchantments, my Webb, around Noah, and you.

Let fate do her worst ! we have laid up enough ;
Our hay is all made, and the storm may blow rough,
We care not ; why should we ? we've had out our fun,
And never again can they say we're hard run.
Long, long may our hearts with such comforts be stored,
Like pockets wherein jingling coin has been poured.
You may break, you may ruin the Bank, if you will,
But the notes and the specie, will hang round us still.

BANK MELODY—No. V.

Air.—"John Anderson, my jo, John."

Nick Biddle, O! my auld Nick,
　　When we were first acquent,
The Bank had full five years to run,
　　The fees were freely *lent ;*
But now the Bank is winding up,
　　The cash don't come so thick
But blessings on your silver pow,
　　Nick Biddle, my auld Nick !

Nick Biddle, O! my auld Nick,
　　We've had our fun thegither,
Money and canty days, Nick,
　　We've spent wi' ane anither ;
Now we maun totter down, Nick,
　　But hand in hand we'll stick,
And growl thegither at the foot,
　　Nick Biddle, oh! my Nick.

19*

BANK MELODY—No. VI.

GULIAN'S FEAST.

" Fill the goblet again ; for I never before
   Felt the joy, that now kindles my heart to its core :
   Let us drink :—who would not ? since through life's-varied round,
   In the goblet alone, *no deception is found.*"—BYRON.

'T was at the Castle feast, of beer, and fun,
   That great Verplanck had won.
   High on a stage of cedar,
   Sat the elected leader,
   Beneath a tow cloth canopy, to ward the sun ;
      A shining steeple ;
   A moral weathercock, above the gaping people.
   Phil H——ne, and Webb, and Glentworth stood around,
   Their skulls, with wigs, and scalps, and scratches
         bound :
   So should success in politics be crowned.
         The new appointed street inspectors,
      . Mix'd, hob-a-nob, with bank directors ;
         While smirking, honest Mr. Bull
         Of pleasure filled the chalice full.——
         Happy, happy, happy Mayor ?
               None but the wigs,
               None but the wigs,
   None but the wigs surround thy chair !

Joe Hoxie mid the throng,
High pitch'd his tuneful voice,
And warbled many a song,
Appropriate, and choice.
The trembling notes, like Nick's pervade the land,
And win for Joe the vote of many a hand.
He sung Kentucky's trump-card son,
Who, tonguey, went to Washington ;—
Such is the power of mighty gold
On lawyers getting old !
A Senator's grave form belied the attorney ;
Sublime, on rail road cars, he took his journey,
When first he woed the beauteous Bank,
And lowly bending, knelt to thank
The generous hand that *images* had sent him,
Sovereigns that reign o'er all the world had lent him
The listening wigs look on with kindling eye ;
" Hurra for Clay ! hurrah ! hurrah !" they cry :
" The day is ours ! Verplanck and Victory !"

With tickled ears
The chairman hears,
And drinks the sound
That floats around,
As if it were the music of the spheres.

The praise of Webster next,
Joe pitched on for his text,
The god-like man is hovering here !
A foaming bumper now of beer !
Hand around the mugs there, Stillwell,
See that all the wig boys fill well.

Again! again! fill—fill!
Nick Biddle pays the bill.
  'T was honest Wester's patriotic voice
  Approved it vile, and wicked to rejoice
At the victories won by soldier and tar,
In a shameful immoral war.

Warmed by the song, Verplanck grew vain,
Fought all the election o'er again,
And thrice he proved that loss of votes, was most un-
    doubted gain.
Joe marked the Wig Mayor getting " high·;"
His threatening arm, his bloodshot eye ;
And prudently, therefore, changed the tune,
To the mournful air of " Bonnie Doon."
  He sang John Quincy great and learned !
   By too severe a fate
Fallen ! fallen ! fallen ! fallen !
Fallen from his high estate,
By fickle fortune spurned !
Gone his light houses in the skies,
He pleads distress, and groans and sighs.
Nor e'en a barren, solitary hope has,
Nor boasts his once loved Ebony and Topaz.
     " Enough—forbear,"
     Sung out the Mayor,
     Getting into a huff ;
    " We had quite enough
    Of that sorrowful stuff,
Give us something funny, like ' Barney Brallaghan,'
I've called for that once—shall I have, sir, to call
  again ?"

Joe liked not this wipe,
But he pitched his pipe,
Like a dutiful wig, to the praise of beer,
And comfort poured on the wig Mayor's ear;
'T 'was but a kindred spirit to beget,
For heavy sorrow always loves a wet.

Jews harp like, in Yankee measures,
Soon he twanged his soul to pleasures.
Office he sung, is, toil, and trouble,
Honor but an empty bubble
Soon the official term is out,
And then you're back with the rabble rout.
If in office there's no comfort,
Kill your care, by taking rum for't!
There the bottle stands, beside thee,
Take the goods the Gods provide thee.
The listening clerks "encore" and cry "bravo,"
"Well sung, hurrah! bravo! hurrah for Joe!"

The Mayor unable to resist,
Took the decanter in his fist,
And pulled and breathed, pulled and breathed,
Pulled and breathed, and pulled again:
At length, when he had got enough of liquor, he
Fell prostrate on the stage, and tumbling cursed
old Hickory!

Now at him, Joe, again!
Scream it you cripple, with a savage strain!
Tell him the Bank is broke;—the Bank!
Nick Biddle's "burst"! awake Verplanck!

Hark! Hark!—The horrid sound
Has raised up his head,
As awaked from the dead,
And amazed he stares around!
To the Arsenal! red Fisher cries—
See *Erinnys* arise!
No wig does she wear,
But her natural hair,
Blast her eyes!

Behold a ghastly band
With shillalah each in hand!
These are Irish ghosts that fell by the dirks
Of the valiant Merchant' clerks!
Be ready to fly
If they catch your eye;
Behold! how they brandish their clubs on high,
How they point to the old sixth ward,
And the bristling arsenal yard!
They come! They come! the spirit crew—
Stop singing, Joe!—what the Devil shall we do!
" I'm off," said the Mayor, " if wrong I ask pardon ;"—
And so broke up the feast at Castle Garden.

BANK MELODY—No. VII.

AN ODE TO YOUNG NICK.

> " Quo, inter syngrapha,
> Premis, insoluta——"
>
> *Cyp. Torrent. Carm. XXII.**

WHITHER, midst falling due
And unpaid notes of Webster, Sprague, and Clay,
Far, through thy subject states, dost thou pursue
    Thy autocratic way?

    Vainly, the pauper's prayers
Borne on the winds unsavory arise ;
What matter is it how the rascal fares ?
    No ; laugh, and d——n his eyes.

    See'st thou the palace proud,
And princely towers frowning on the lea,
And Mammon throned, with serfs, a lowly crowd,
    Bending the trembling knee ?

    There is a power, whose care,
Blood-bought, upholds thee tyrant of the land,
And he has tamed, O Nick ! the prince of air—
    Behemoth, to thy hand.

---

* Cyprianus Torrentius, was a lyric poet of great merit, though little
noticed, who flourished about 200, A. C. His works are all lost except the

Long years, thy rod hath ruled
The meagre fortunes of the rabble rout,
And still thy ingrate enemies are fooled,
    Although thy lease is out.

But soon that reign shall cease ;
Soon shall thy paper sceptre pass away,
Soon shalt thou hear the cry, " I'll have my lease,
    And bond," and curse the day.

BANK   MELODY—No. VIII.

YE seamen of Columbia
That guard our native seas,
Whose flag has braved, and triumphed in
The battle and the breeze !
Your own good *Standard* now run up
To match another foe !
And roll to the poll
While the stormy tempests blow ;
While the battle rages loud and long
And the stormy tempests blow !

Ode, of which the above is a literal translation.   This is fortunately preserved in the treatise of Tertullianus " de Lyricis," written shortly after
his conversion to christiany.   The commencement of it may be found in
St. Jerome's famous letter to Tertullian, where it is quoted with ecomias-
tic comment.   Bryant has transferred the thought and style of the poem
to his " Ode to a Water Fowl," without giving credit to the original.
This was, no doubt, an accidental omission, or else, perhaps, it is another
proof of the truth of the old maxim, that " good poets hire out their souls
to the same sort of tenants."

The spirits of your fathers
Are calling you to rise !
Your country's ship thumps on a *Bank*,
And loud your captain cries !
The shade of gallant Lawrence, men,
Will make each bosom glow ;
As you roll to the poll
While Nick Biddle's lawyers blow,
While the battle rages loud and long,
And old Nick's lawyers blow.

Columbia needs no monarch,
No *banks* along her coast ;
She owns no pampered money king,
For freedom is her boast ?
For Lawrence, then, blue jackets all,
Against the Bank we'll row,
And they'll roar, on the shore,
When they see Nick puff and blow ;
While the battle rages loud and long
And the stormy tempests blow.

The stars and stripes of freedom
Shall yet terriffic float—
Your standard sheet shall stream until
You've sunk Nick Biddle's boat.
Then, then, ye ocean-voters
Our song and feast shall flow
To the fame of your name.
When old Nick has ceased to blow
When the 'Tory cry is heard no more,
And the bank has ceased to blow.

BANK MELODY—No. IX.

BURIAL OF THE RIGHT HON. MRS. BANK.

Not a speech was heard, not a Lawyer's tongue,
  As we raised the shrunk corse to our shoulders ;
Not a stave of distress, not a melody sung
  O'er the ditch where the old lady moulders.

We buried her privately, late at night,
  In a lone bye place ; Major Downing
" Vow'd by jings, that he never yet see such a sight,"
  And he called it " a judgment crownen."

No heaped up mound, nor vault we tricked ;
  But splash ! in the water we pitched her,
And she raised up her head, and grunted, and kicked,
  As if the old boy had bewitched her.

Hal Clay said a prayer ; it was rather brief;
  He was so overcome with sorrow ;
And we all more or less, had a touch of grief,
  For we knew what would come on the morrow.

We knew—as we laid the old woman down,
  For the mummies and eels to feed on—
That her goods and effects were to go to the town,
  As had early in life been agreed on.

We knew that we all had to settle our loans,
　　That the time had gone by for renewal,
That the Demos would laugh at our sighs and groans,
　　And the sheriff be callous and cruel.

We had just got done, and we stood in the damp,
　　And were talking about absconding ;
When we heard the deputy tipstaff's tramp,
　　And the marshal's voice resounding.

Quicker than lightning, we all cleared out,
　　And we cursed every Troglodyte Tory ;
Not a line did *we* write, not a speech did we spout.
　　But we left her all alone with her glory.

END OF VOL. II.

14 DAY USE

RETURN TO DESK FROM WHICH BORROW

This book is due on the last date stamped below
on the date to which renewed.
Renewed books are subject to immediate recal

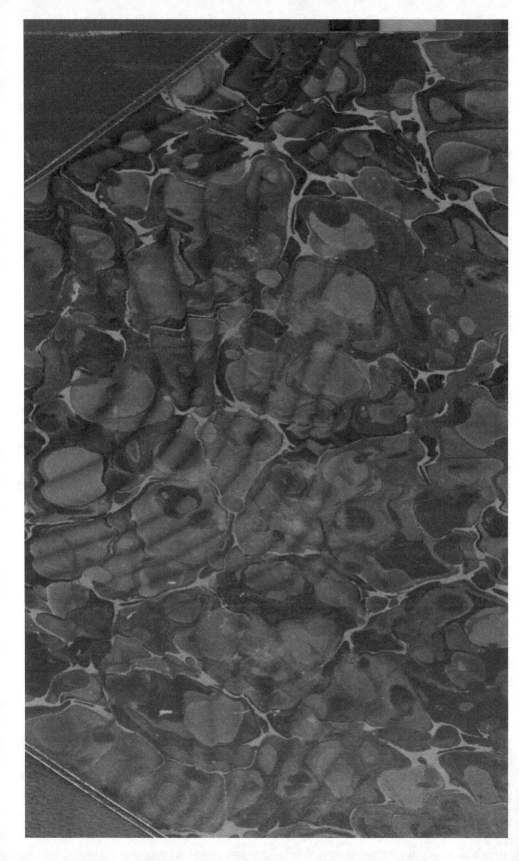

CPSIA information can be obtained
at www.ICGtesting.com
Printed in the USA
BVHW041518160819
556068BV00022B/2554/P